HMH

math expressions

Dr. Karen C. Fuson

Watch the frog come alive in its pond as you discover and solve math challenges.

Download the *Math Worlds AR* app available on Android or iOS devices.

Grade 1
Volume 2

This material is based upon work supported by the **National Science Foundation** under Grant Numbers ESI-9816320, REC-9806020, and RED-935373.

Any opinions, findings, and conclusions, or recommendations expressed in this material are those of the author and do not necessarily reflect the views of the National Science Foundation.

BIG IDEA 1 - Teen Solution Methods

BIG IDEA 2 - Find Patterns and Relationships

© Houghton Mifflin Harcourt Publishing Company

BIG IDEA 1 - Tell and Write Time

BIG IDEA 2 - Shapes and Equal Shares

BIG IDEA 3 - Measure and Order by Length

Unit 8 | Two-Digit Addition

BIG IDEA - Add 2-Digit Numbers

Student Resources

Dear Family:

In the previous unit, your child learned the Make a Ten strategy to find teen totals. Now, your child builds on previous knowledge to use make a ten to find an unknown partner. The Make a Ten strategy is explained below.

In a teen addition problem such as 9 + 5, children break apart the lesser number to make a ten with the greater number. Because 9 + 1 = 10, they break apart 5 into 1 + 4. Then they add the extra 4 onto 10 to find the total. A similar method is used to find unknown partners with teen totals. Children look for ways to make a ten because it is easier to add onto 10.

In the *Math Expressions* program, Make-a-Ten Cards help children use this method. Each card has a problem on the front. The back shows the answer and illustrates the Make a Ten strategy using pictures of dots. Below the pictures are corresponding numbers to help children understand how to make a ten. Practice the method with your child. As you continue to practice the Make a Ten strategy with your child, your child will become more adept at using mental math.

If you have any questions about the Make a Ten strategy, please contact me.

Sincerely,
Your child's teacher

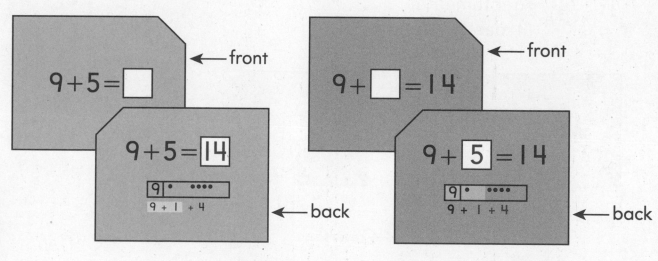

Make-a-Ten Cards

Estimada familia:

En la unidad anterior, su niño aprendió la Estrategia hacer decenas para hallar totales de números de 11 a 19. Ahora, su niño ampliará esos conocimientos previos y hará decenas para hallar una parte desconocida. La Estrategia hacer decenas se explica debajo.

En una suma con números de 11 a 19, tal como 9 + 5, los niños separan el número menor para formar una decena con el número mayor. Como 9 + 1 = 10, separan el 5 en 1 + 4. Luego suman al 10 los 4 que sobran para hallar el total. Un método semejante se usa para hallar partes desconocidas con totales de números de 11 a 19. Los niños buscan maneras de formar una decena porque es más fácil sumar con 10.

En el programa *Math Expressions* las tarjetas de hacer decenas ayudan a los niños a usar este método. Cada tarjeta tiene un problema en el frente. En el reverso se muestra la respuesta y se ilustra la Estrategia hacer decenas mediante dibujos de puntos. Debajo de los dibujos están los números correspondientes para ayudar a los niños a comprender cómo se hace una decena. Practique el método con su niño. A medida que practican la estrategia, su niño adquirirá mayor dominio del cálculo mental.

Si tiene alguna pregunta sobre la Estrategia hacer decenas, por favor comuníquese conmigo.

Atentamente,
El maestro de su niño

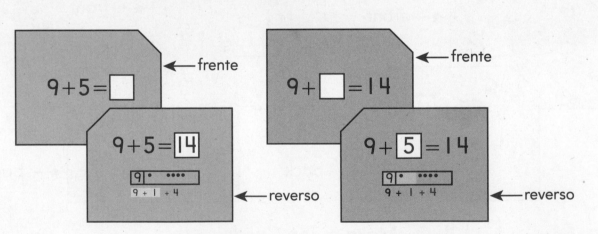

Tarjetas de hacer decenas

10-group	longest
column	number line
grid	row

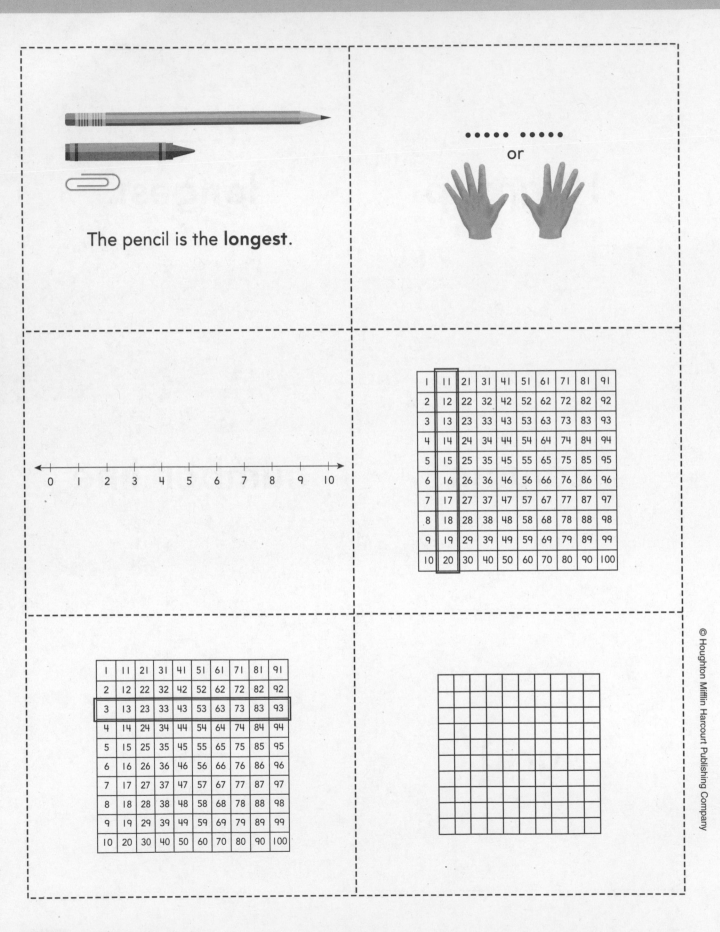

The pencil is the **longest**.

or

1	11	21	31	41	51	61	71	81	91
2	12	22	32	42	52	62	72	82	92
3	13	23	33	43	53	63	73	83	93
4	14	24	34	44	54	64	74	84	94
5	15	25	35	45	55	65	75	85	95
6	16	26	36	46	56	66	76	86	96
7	17	27	37	47	57	67	77	87	97
8	18	28	38	48	58	68	78	88	98
9	19	29	39	49	59	69	79	89	99
10	20	30	40	50	60	70	80	90	100

1	11	21	31	41	51	61	71	81	91
2	12	22	32	42	52	62	72	82	92
3	13	23	33	43	53	63	73	83	93
4	14	24	34	44	54	64	74	84	94
5	15	25	35	45	55	65	75	85	95
6	16	26	36	46	56	66	76	86	96
7	17	27	37	47	57	67	77	87	97
8	18	28	38	48	58	68	78	88	98
9	19	29	39	49	59	69	79	89	99
10	20	30	40	50	60	70	80	90	100

shortest

The paper clip is the **shortest**.

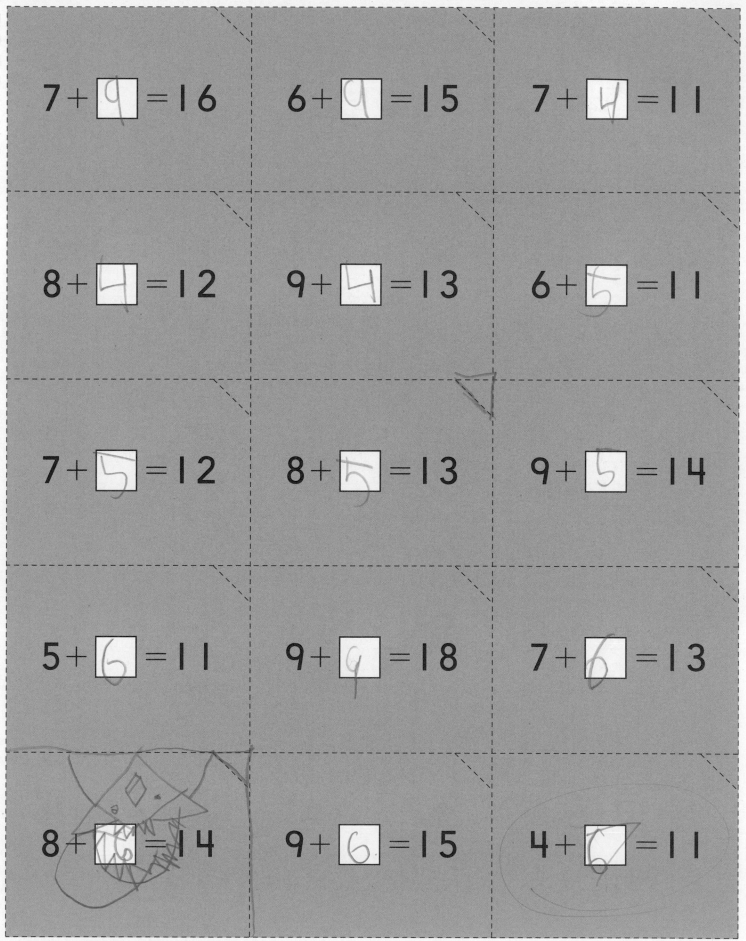

$7 + \boxed{9} = 16$

$6 + \boxed{9} = 15$

$7 + \boxed{4} = 11$

$8 + \boxed{4} = 12$

$9 + \boxed{4} = 13$

$6 + \boxed{5} = 11$

$7 + \boxed{5} = 12$

$8 + \boxed{5} = 13$

$9 + \boxed{5} = 14$

$5 + \boxed{6} = 11$

$9 + \boxed{9} = 18$

$7 + \boxed{6} = 13$

$8 + \boxed{6} = 14$

$9 + \boxed{6} = 15$

$4 + \boxed{7} = 11$

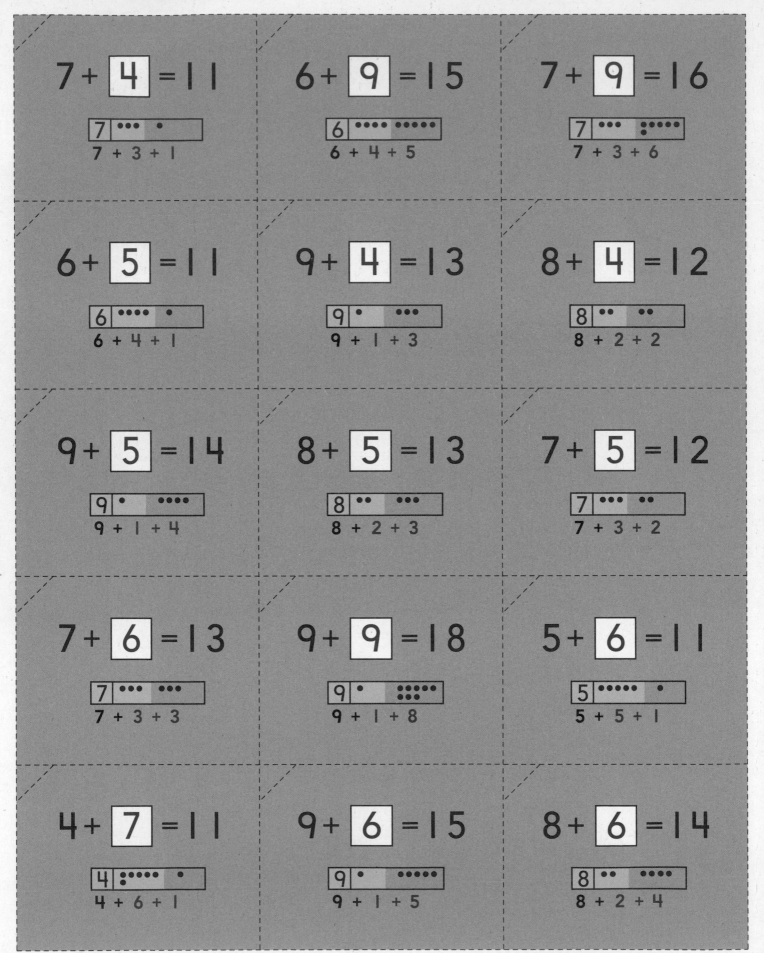

$7 + \boxed{4} = 11$

7 | ••• •

7 + 3 + 1

$6 + \boxed{9} = 15$

6 | •••• •••••

6 + 4 + 5

$7 + \boxed{9} = 16$

7 | ••• ••••••

7 + 3 + 6

$6 + \boxed{5} = 11$

6 | •••• •

6 + 4 + 1

$9 + \boxed{4} = 13$

9 | • •••

9 + 1 + 3

$8 + \boxed{4} = 12$

8 | •• ••

8 + 2 + 2

$9 + \boxed{5} = 14$

9 | • ••••

9 + 1 + 4

$8 + \boxed{5} = 13$

8 | •• •••

8 + 2 + 3

$7 + \boxed{5} = 12$

7 | ••• ••

7 + 3 + 2

$7 + \boxed{6} = 13$

7 | ••• •••

7 + 3 + 3

$9 + \boxed{9} = 18$

9 | • ••••••••

9 + 1 + 8

$5 + \boxed{6} = 11$

5 | ••••• •

5 + 5 + 1

$4 + \boxed{7} = 11$

4 | •••••• •

4 + 6 + 1

$9 + \boxed{6} = 15$

9 | • •••••

9 + 1 + 5

$8 + \boxed{6} = 14$

8 | •• ••••

8 + 2 + 4

Purple Make-a-Ten Cards

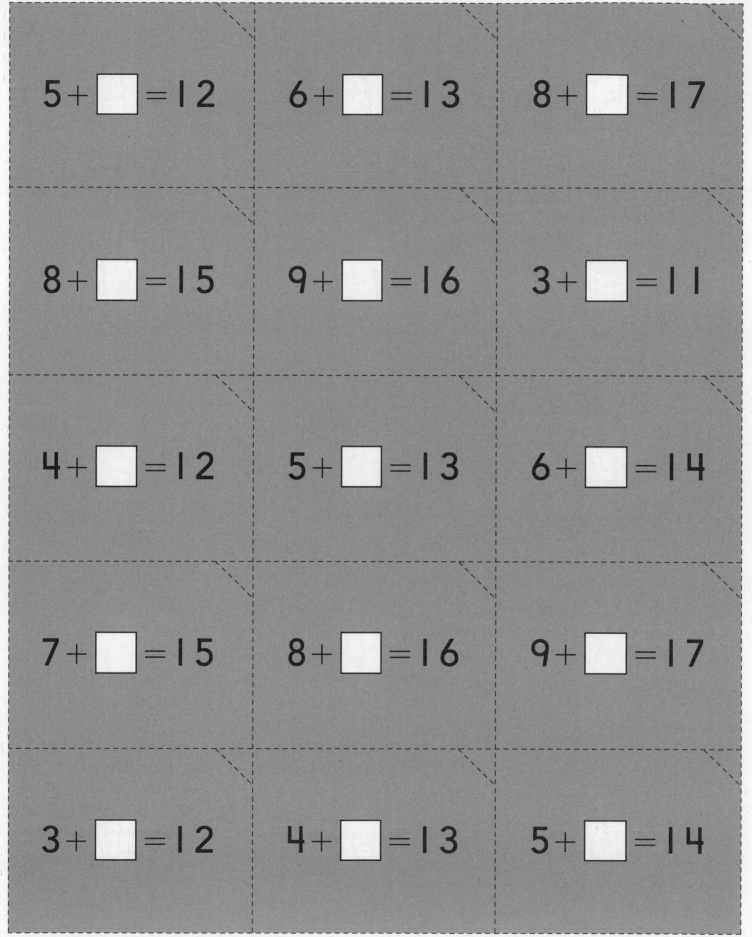

5 + ☐ = 12   6 + ☐ = 13   8 + ☐ = 17

8 + ☐ = 15   9 + ☐ = 16   3 + ☐ = 11

4 + ☐ = 12   5 + ☐ = 13   6 + ☐ = 14

7 + ☐ = 15   8 + ☐ = 16   9 + ☐ = 17

3 + ☐ = 12   4 + ☐ = 13   5 + ☐ = 14

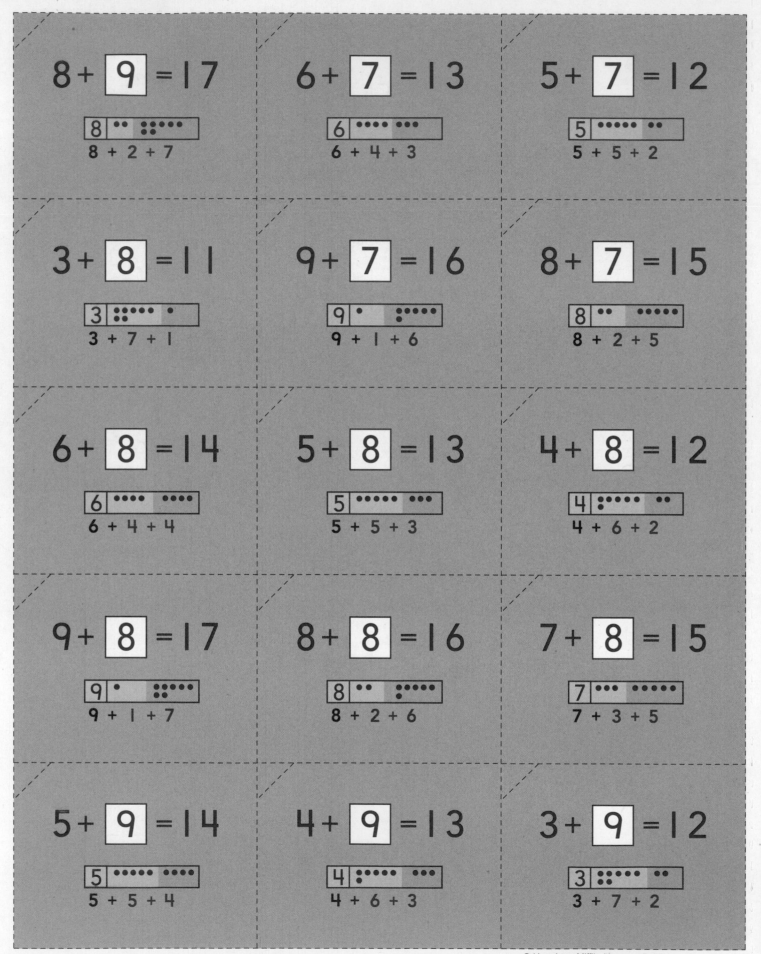

$8 + \boxed{9} = 17$

8 | •• •••••
8 + 2 + 7

$6 + \boxed{7} = 13$

6 | •••• •••
6 + 4 + 3

$5 + \boxed{7} = 12$

5 | ••••• ••
5 + 5 + 2

$3 + \boxed{8} = 11$

3 | ••••• •
3 + 7 + 1

$9 + \boxed{7} = 16$

9 | • ••••••
9 + 1 + 6

$8 + \boxed{7} = 15$

8 | •• •••••
8 + 2 + 5

$6 + \boxed{8} = 14$

6 | •••• ••••
6 + 4 + 4

$5 + \boxed{8} = 13$

5 | ••••• •••
5 + 5 + 3

$4 + \boxed{8} = 12$

4 | •••• ••
4 + 6 + 2

$9 + \boxed{8} = 17$

9 | • •••••••
9 + 1 + 7

$8 + \boxed{8} = 16$

8 | •• ••••••
8 + 2 + 6

$7 + \boxed{8} = 15$

7 | ••• •••••
7 + 3 + 5

$5 + \boxed{9} = 14$

5 | ••••• ••••
5 + 5 + 4

$4 + \boxed{9} = 13$

4 | ••••• •••
4 + 6 + 3

$3 + \boxed{9} = 12$

3 | ••••• ••
3 + 7 + 2

Purple Make-a-Ten Cards

Name _____

Match the equation with the picture that shows
how to use the Make a Ten strategy to solve.
Write the unknown partner.

1 8 + [4] = 12

2 9 + [6] = 15

3 7 + [5] = 12

4 8 + [6] = 14

5 9 + [3] = 12

6 8 + [7] = 15

7 9 + [2] = 11

8 9 + [8] = 17

9 7 + [4] = 11

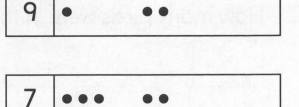
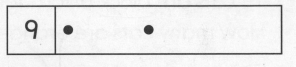

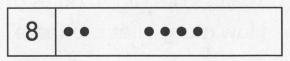
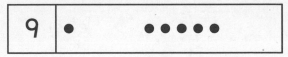
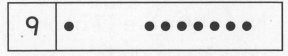

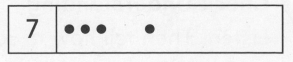
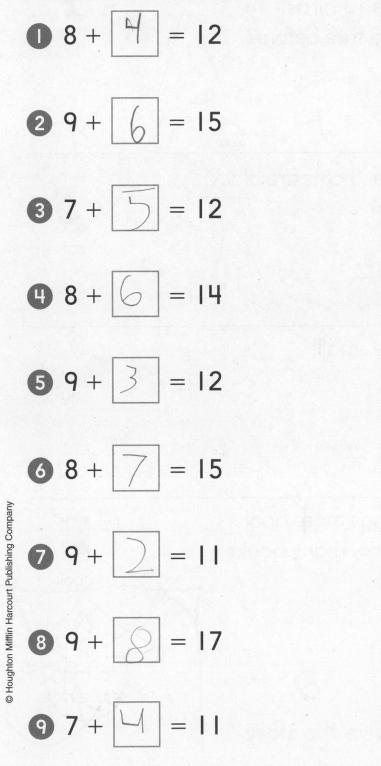

Unknown Partners with Teen Totals **229**

Solve the story problem.

**Show your work.
Use drawings, numbers, or words.**

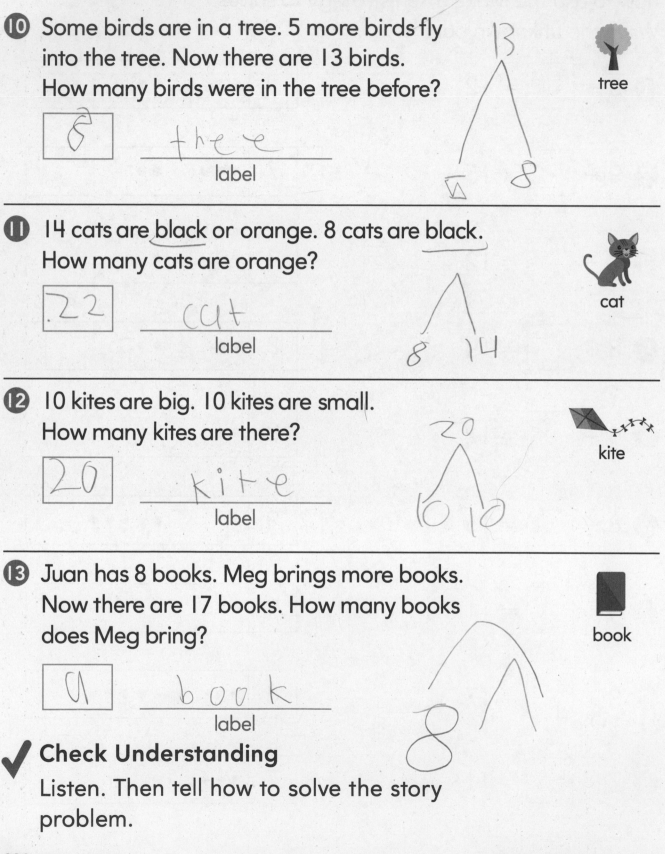

10 Some birds are in a tree. 5 more birds fly into the tree. Now there are 13 birds. How many birds were in the tree before?

8

three
label

13
5   8

tree

11 14 cats are black or orange. 8 cats are black. How many cats are orange?

22

cat
label

8   14

cat

12 10 kites are big. 10 kites are small. How many kites are there?

20

kite
label

20
10   10

kite

13 Juan has 8 books. Meg brings more books. Now there are 17 books. How many books does Meg bring?

9

book
label

8

book

✔ **Check Understanding**

Listen. Then tell how to solve the story problem.

Unknown Partners with Teen Totals

15 − 6 = ☐   16 − 7 = ☐   11 − 7 = ☐

12 − 8 = ☐   13 − 9 = ☐   11 − 6 = ☐

12 − 7 = ☐   13 − 8 = ☐   14 − 9 = ☐

11 − 5 = ☐   17 − 8 = ☐   13 − 7 = ☐

14 − 8 = ☐   15 − 9 = ☐   11 − 4 = ☐

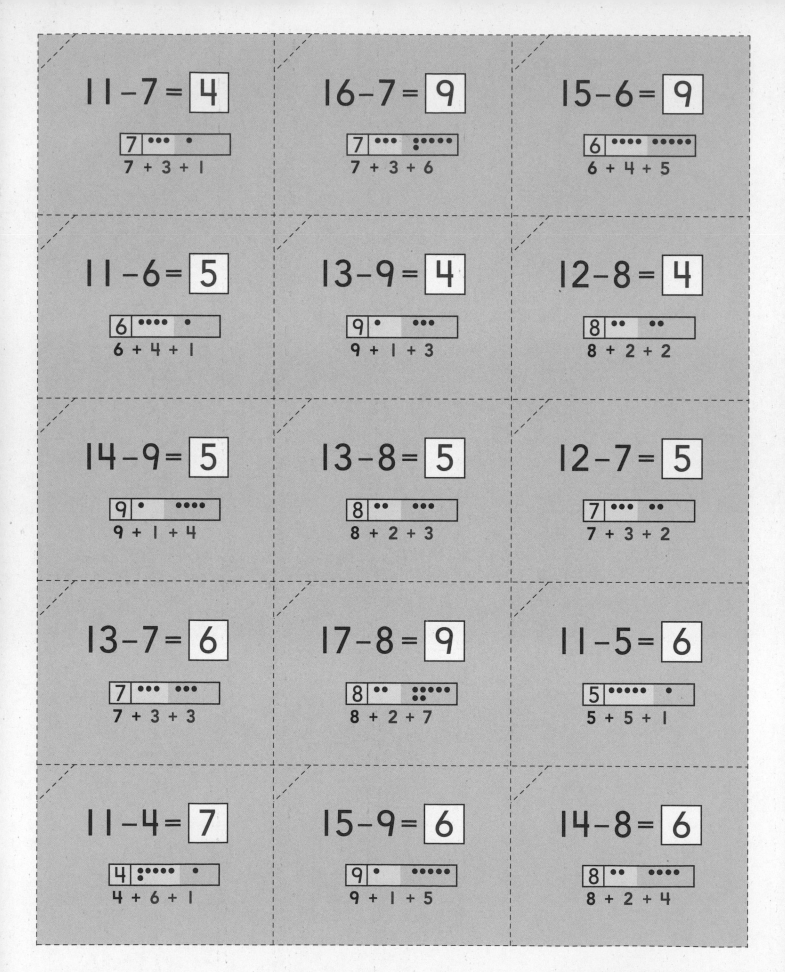

11 − 7 = 4
7 + 3 + 1

16 − 7 = 9
7 + 3 + 6

15 − 6 = 9
6 + 4 + 5

11 − 6 = 5
6 + 4 + 1

13 − 9 = 4
9 + 1 + 3

12 − 8 = 4
8 + 2 + 2

14 − 9 = 5
9 + 1 + 4

13 − 8 = 5
8 + 2 + 3

12 − 7 = 5
7 + 3 + 2

13 − 7 = 6
7 + 3 + 3

17 − 8 = 9
8 + 2 + 7

11 − 5 = 6
5 + 5 + 1

11 − 4 = 7
4 + 6 + 1

15 − 9 = 6
9 + 1 + 5

14 − 8 = 6
8 + 2 + 4

Blue Make-a-Ten Cards

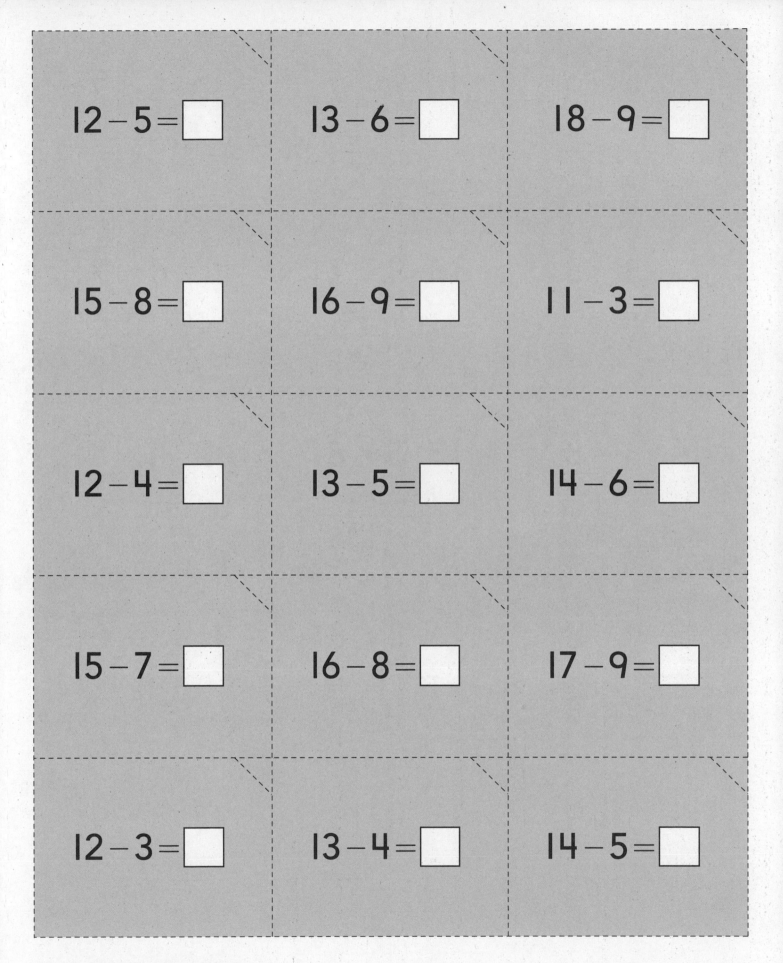

12 − 5 = ☐   13 − 6 = ☐   18 − 9 = ☐

15 − 8 = ☐   16 − 9 = ☐   11 − 3 = ☐

12 − 4 = ☐   13 − 5 = ☐   14 − 6 = ☐

15 − 7 = ☐   16 − 8 = ☐   17 − 9 = ☐

12 − 3 = ☐   13 − 4 = ☐   14 − 5 = ☐

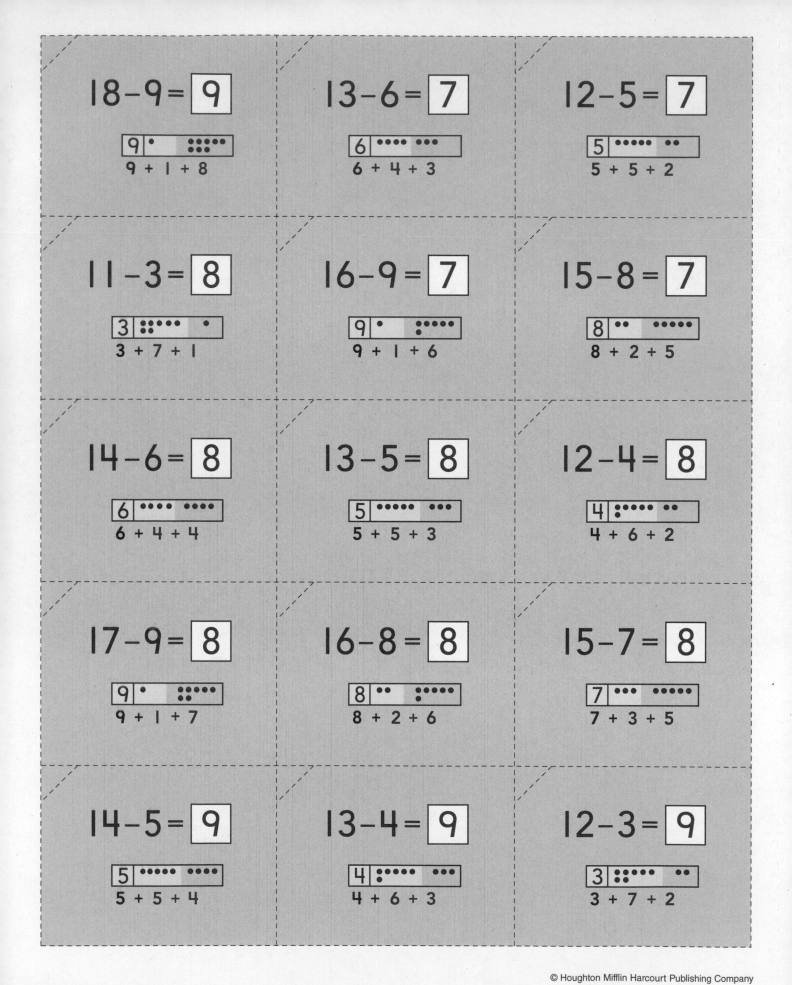

18 − 9 = 9
9 + 1 + 8

13 − 6 = 7
6 + 4 + 3

12 − 5 = 7
5 + 5 + 2

11 − 3 = 8
3 + 7 + 1

16 − 9 = 7
9 + 1 + 6

15 − 8 = 7
8 + 2 + 5

14 − 6 = 8
6 + 4 + 4

13 − 5 = 8
5 + 5 + 3

12 − 4 = 8
4 + 6 + 2

17 − 9 = 8
9 + 1 + 7

16 − 8 = 8
8 + 2 + 6

15 − 7 = 8
7 + 3 + 5

14 − 5 = 9
5 + 5 + 4

13 − 4 = 9
4 + 6 + 3

12 − 3 = 9
3 + 7 + 2

Blue Make-a-Ten Cards

Name _____

Match the equation with the picture that shows how to use the Make a Ten strategy to solve.

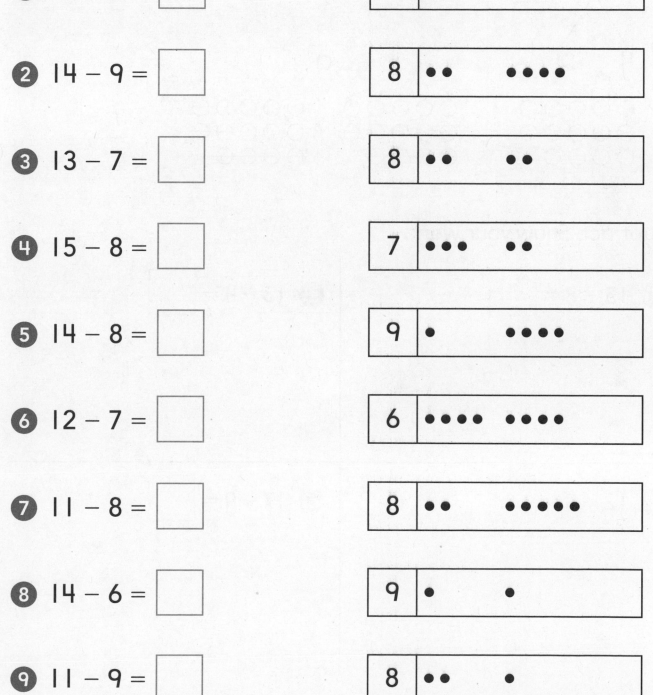

1 $12 - 8 = \boxed{}$ | 7 | ••• ••• |

2 $14 - 9 = \boxed{}$ | 8 | •• •••• |

3 $13 - 7 = \boxed{}$ | 8 | •• •• |

4 $15 - 8 = \boxed{}$ | 7 | ••• •• |

5 $14 - 8 = \boxed{}$ | 9 | • •••• |

6 $12 - 7 = \boxed{}$ | 6 | •••• •••• |

7 $11 - 8 = \boxed{}$ | 8 | •• ••••• |

8 $14 - 6 = \boxed{}$ | 9 | • • |

9 $11 - 9 = \boxed{}$ | 8 | •• • |

Subtraction with Teen Numbers **235**

$14 - 6 = \boxed{8}$

4   2

	Step 1	Step 2
	$14 - 4 = 10$	$10 - 2 = 8$

Subtract. Show your work.

10 $15 - 8 = \boxed{}$

11 $13 - 4 = \boxed{}$

12 $12 - 9 = \boxed{}$

13 $17 - 9 = \boxed{}$

✓ **Check Understanding**

Draw to show how to make a ten to solve $13 - 8$.

Subtraction with Teen Numbers

Name _____

Solve the story problem. **Show your work.**
Use drawings, numbers, or words.

1 17 berries are in a bowl. 9 are red and the rest are purple. How many berries are purple?

bowl

[ ] _____
label

2 I draw some stars. 8 are large and 7 are small. How many stars do I draw?

star

[ ] _____
label

3 There are 14 puppies. Some are brown and some are black. How many brown and black puppies could there be?
Show three answers.

puppy

[ ] brown puppies and [ ] black puppies

or [ ] brown puppies and [ ] black puppies

or [ ] brown puppies and [ ] black puppies

© Houghton Mifflin Harcourt Publishing Company

Mixed Practice with Teen Problems **237**

Solve the story problem.

Show your work.
Use drawings, numbers, or words.

4 15 frogs are by the pond. 9 hop away.
How many frogs are there now?

pond

[ ] _____
          label

5 16 butterflies are in the garden.
Some fly away. There are 8 left.
How many butterflies fly away?

butterflies

[ ] _____
          label

6 Some grapes are in a bowl. I eat 6 of them.
Now there are 7 grapes. How many grapes
were in the bowl before?

grapes

[ ] _____
          label

7 There are 12 horses in a field. Some run
away. Now there are 5 horses. How many
horses run away?

horse

[ ] _____
          label

✓ **Check Understanding**

Listen to the story problem. Then explain
how to solve it.

Mixed Practice with Teen Problems

Name _____

Match the equation with the picture that shows
how to use the Make a Ten strategy to solve.

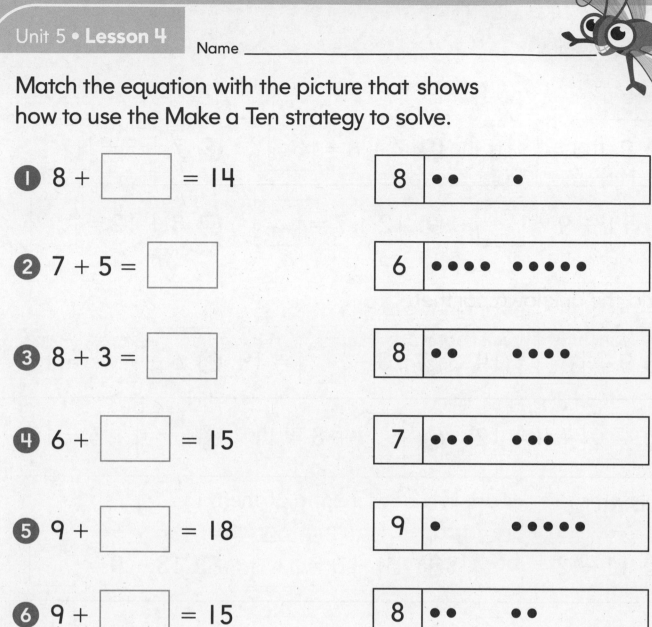

1 8 + ⬜ = 14

2 7 + 5 = ⬜

3 8 + 3 = ⬜

4 6 + ⬜ = 15

5 9 + ⬜ = 18

6 9 + ⬜ = 15

7 8 + 4 = ⬜

8 7 + 6 = ⬜

9 Ring the picture above that shows
how to use the Make a Ten strategy
to solve the equation.

13 − 7 = ⬜

Small Group Practice with Teen Problems **239**

Add.

10 $9 + 3 = \boxed{}$ **11** $7 + 8 = \boxed{}$ **12** $7 + 5 = \boxed{}$

13 $11 + 9 = \boxed{}$ **14** $12 + 7 = \boxed{}$ **15** $8 + 12 = \boxed{}$

Find the unknown partner.

16 $9 + \boxed{} = 14$ **17** $10 + \boxed{} = 19$ **18** $6 + \boxed{} = 13$

19 $\boxed{} + 4 = 12$ **20** $\boxed{} + 8 = 11$ **21** $\boxed{} + 6 = 15$

Subtract.

22 $11 - 2 = \boxed{}$ **23** $14 - 6 = \boxed{}$ **24** $13 - 9 = \boxed{}$

25 $16 - 8 = \boxed{}$ **26** $13 - 7 = \boxed{}$ **27** $12 - 5 = \boxed{}$

PATH to FLUENCY Subtract.

1 $10 - 8 = \boxed{}$ **2** $7 - 1 = \boxed{}$ **3** $6 - 6 = \boxed{}$

4 $9 - 7 = \boxed{}$ **5** $8 - 4 = \boxed{}$ **6** $10 - 6 = \boxed{}$

✔ **Check Understanding**

Explain how to make ten to solve. $17 - 8 = \boxed{}$

Small Group Practice with Teen Problems

Name _____

1 Rosa reads 8 stories. Tim reads 5 stories.
How many stories do they read in all?

2 Rosa reads 8 stories. Tim also reads some stories.
They read 13 stories in all. How many stories
does Tim read?

3 Rosa reads some stories. Tim reads 5 stories. They read 13
stories in all. How many stories does Rosa read?

© Houghton Mifflin Harcourt Publishing Company

Teen Problems with Various Unknowns **241**

Some crayons are in a box.
I take 6 crayons out.
Now there are 9 crayons in the box.
How many crayons were in the box before?

Am I correct?

4 Look at what Puzzled Penguin wrote.

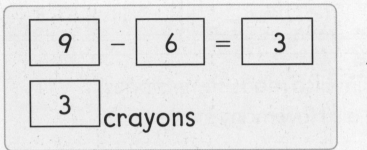

| 9 | – | 6 | = | 3 |

3 crayons

5 Help Puzzled Penguin.

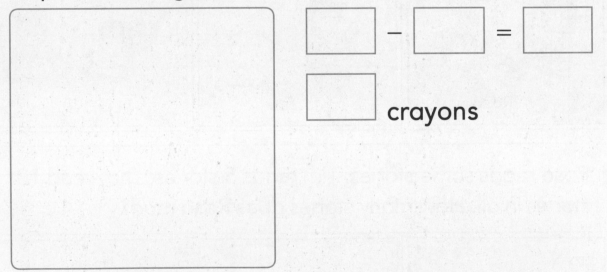

☐ – ☐ = ☐

☐ crayons

✓ **Check Understanding**

Make up a story problem to find the unknown total and another story problem to find an unknown partner.

Teen Problems with Various Unknowns

Name _____

Model and solve the story problem.
Color to show your model.
Cross out the cubes you do not use.

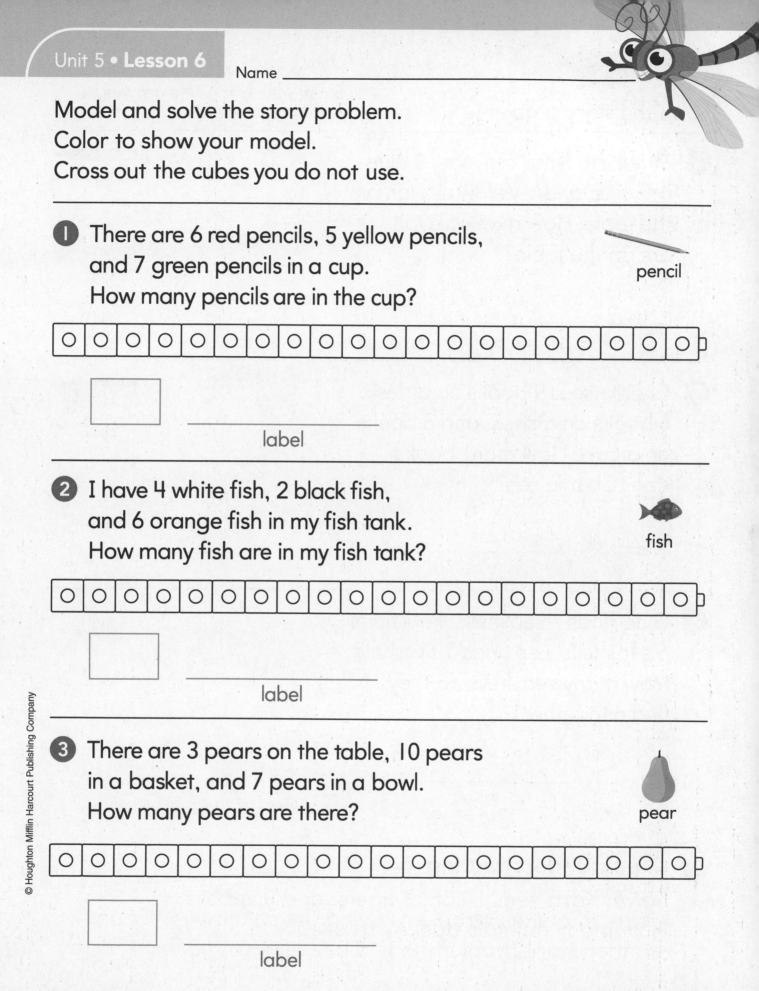

1 There are 6 red pencils, 5 yellow pencils,
and 7 green pencils in a cup.
How many pencils are in the cup?

pencil

label

2 I have 4 white fish, 2 black fish,
and 6 orange fish in my fish tank.
How many fish are in my fish tank?

fish

label

3 There are 3 pears on the table, 10 pears
in a basket, and 7 pears in a bowl.
How many pears are there?

pear

label

Problems with Three Addends **243**

Solve the story problem.

Show your work. Use drawings, numbers, or words.

4 There are 5 red crayons, 9 blue crayons, and 1 yellow crayon on the table. How many crayons are on the table?

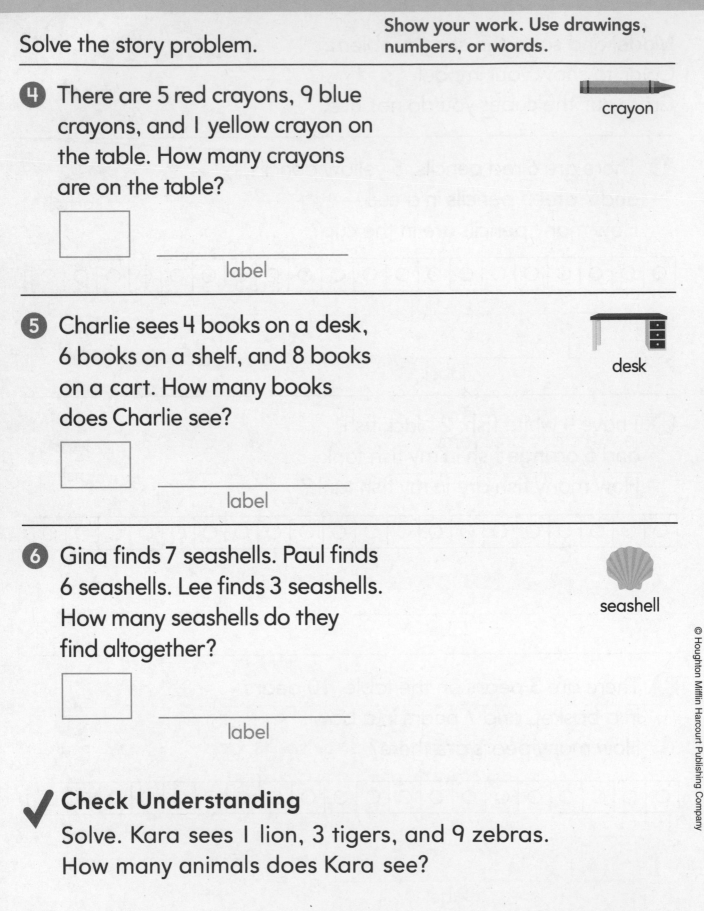

crayon

_____
label

5 Charlie sees 4 books on a desk, 6 books on a shelf, and 8 books on a cart. How many books does Charlie see?

desk

_____
label

6 Gina finds 7 seashells. Paul finds 6 seashells. Lee finds 3 seashells. How many seashells do they find altogether?

seashell

_____
label

✓ **Check Understanding**

Solve. Kara sees 1 lion, 3 tigers, and 9 zebras. How many animals does Kara see?

Problems with Three Addends

Add or subtract.

1 $9 + \boxed{} = 17$

2 $15 - 8 = \boxed{}$

3 $7 + \boxed{} = 16$

Solve the story problem.   Show your work.

4 There are 14 ants. There are 9 red ants, and the rest are black. How many ants are black?

$\boxed{}$ _____
       label

5 Bailey found 4 clam shells, 5 snail shells, and 6 scallop shells. How many shells did she find in all?

$\boxed{}$ _____
       label

Name _____ Date _____

Subtract.

1 7 − 2 = ☐   **2** 6 − 1 = ☐   **3** 7 − 4 = ☐

4 8 − 5 = ☐   **5** 6 − 3 = ☐   **6** 7 − 7 = ☐

7 8 − 7 = ☐   **8** 9 − 6 = ☐   **9** 6 − 5 = ☐

10 8 − 2 = ☐   **11** 10 − 2 = ☐   **12** 9 − 3 = ☐

13 10 − 10 = ☐   **14** 9 − 8 = ☐   **15** 10 − 4 = ☐

VOCABULARY
10-group

1 Ring **10-groups**. Count by tens and ones.
Write the number.

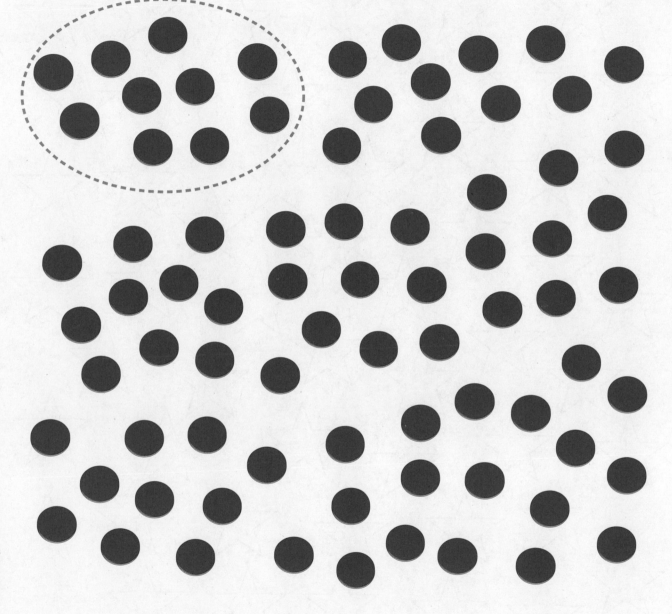

2 Color each 10-group a different color.
Count by tens and ones. Write the number.

✔ **Check Understanding**
Explain how to use tens and ones to
count 95 counters.

Count with Groups of 10

Dear Family:

The next several lessons of this unit build upon what the class learned previously about tens and ones. The Hundred Grid is a tool that allows children to see 10-based patterns in sequence. Seeing numbers in the ordered rows and columns of the Hundred Grid helps children better understand number relationships as they:

- continue to practice with 10-groups, adding tens to any 2-digit number, with totals to 100;
- explore 2-digit subtraction, subtracting tens from decade numbers;
- connect what they know about 10-partners to now find 100-partners.

1	11	21	31	41	51	61	71	81	91
2	12	22	32	42	52	62	72	82	92
3	13	23	33	43	53	63	73	83	93
4	14	24	34	44	54	64	74	84	94
5	15	25	35	45	55	65	75	85	95
6	16	26	36	46	56	66	76	86	96
7	17	27	37	47	57	67	77	87	97
8	18	28	38	48	58	68	78	88	98
9	19	29	39	49	59	69	79	89	99
10	20	30	40	50	60	70	80	90	100

3 ooo
13 | ooo
23 | | ooo
33 | | | ooo
43 | | | | ooo
53 | | | | | ooo
63 | | | | | | ooo
73 | | | | | | | ooo
83 | | | | | | | | ooo
93 | | | | | | | | | ooo

If you have any questions or problems, please contact me.

Sincerely,
Your child's teacher

Estimada familia:

Las siguientes lecciones en esta unidad amplían lo que la clase aprendió anteriormente acerca de decenas y unidades. La Cuadrícula de 100 es un instrumento que permite observar patrones de base 10 en secuencia. Observar los números ordenados en hileras y columnas en la Cuadrícula de 100 ayudará a los niños a comprender mejor la relación entre los números mientras:

• continúan practicando con grupos de 10, sumando decenas a números de 2 dígitos con totales hasta 100;

• exploran la resta de números de 2 dígitos, restando decenas de números que terminan en cero;

• relacionan lo que saben acerca de las partes de 10 para hallar partes de 100.

1	11	21	31	41	51	61	71	81	91
2	12	22	32	42	52	62	72	82	92
3	13	23	33	43	53	63	73	83	93
4	14	24	34	44	54	64	74	84	94
5	15	25	35	45	55	65	75	85	95
6	16	26	36	46	56	66	76	86	96
7	17	27	37	47	57	67	77	87	97
8	18	28	38	48	58	68	78	88	98
9	19	29	39	49	59	69	79	89	99
10	20	30	40	50	60	70	80	90	100

3   ○○○
13 | ○○○
23 || ○○○
33 ||| ○○○
43 |||| ○○○
53 ||||| ○○○
63 ||||| | ○○○
73 ||||| || ○○○
83 ||||| ||| ○○○
93 ||||| |||| ○○○

Si tiene alguna pregunta o algún comentario comuníquese conmigo.

Atentamente,
El maestro de su niño

Name _____

VOCABULARY
column
grid

1 Write the numbers 1–120 in **columns**.

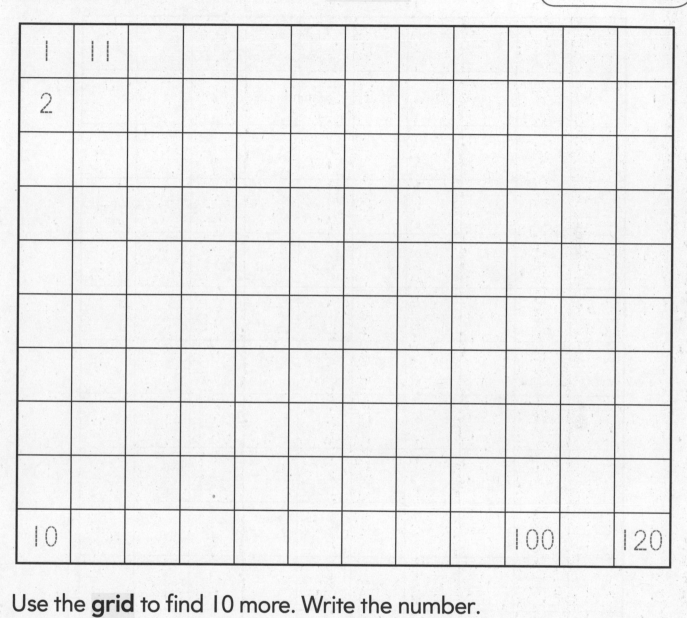

Use the **grid** to find 10 more. Write the number.

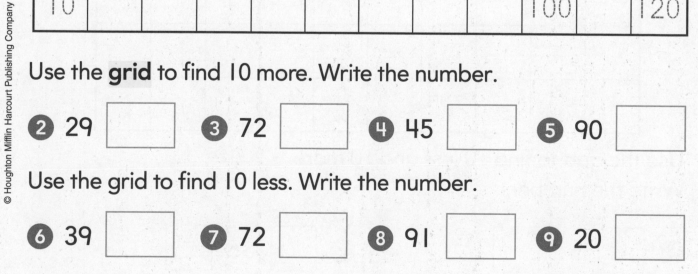

2 29 ☐ **3** 72 ☐ **4** 45 ☐ **5** 90 ☐

Use the grid to find 10 less. Write the number.

6 39 ☐ **7** 72 ☐ **8** 91 ☐ **9** 20 ☐

© Houghton Mifflin Harcourt Publishing Company

10 Write the numbers 1–120 in **rows**.

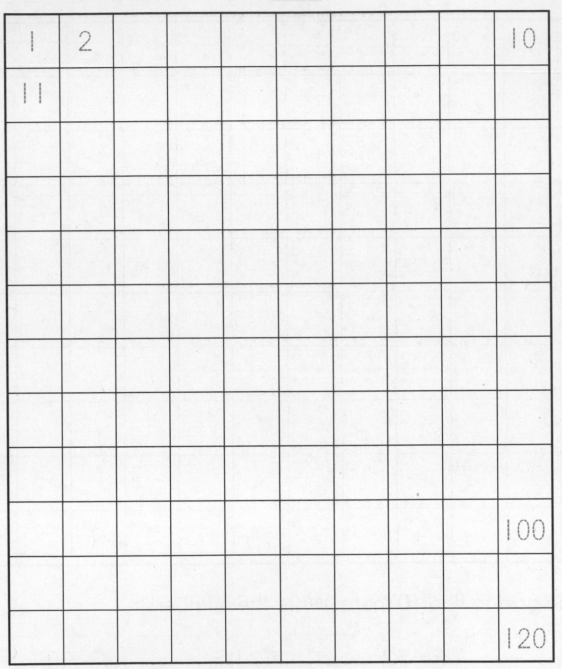

1	2								10
11									
								100	
								120	

Use the grid to find 10 less and 10 more.
Write the numbers.

11 ☐ 51 ☐   **12** ☐ 36 ☐

Name _____

Use the **number line** to count forward or backward. Write the numbers.

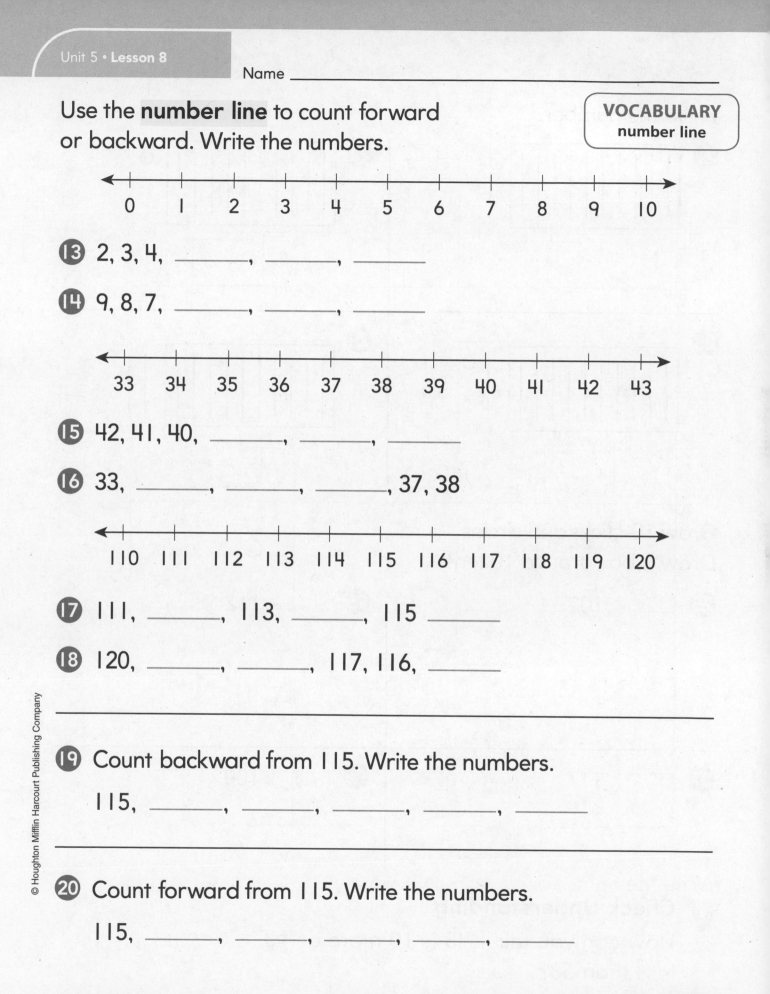

0 1 2 3 4 5 6 7 8 9 10

13 2, 3, 4, _____, _____, _____

14 9, 8, 7, _____, _____, _____

33 34 35 36 37 38 39 40 41 42 43

15 42, 41, 40, _____, _____, _____

16 33, _____, _____, _____, 37, 38

110 111 112 113 114 115 116 117 118 119 120

17 111, _____, 113, _____, 115 _____

18 120, _____, _____, 117, 116, _____

19 Count backward from 115. Write the numbers.

115, _____, _____, _____, _____, _____

20 Count forward from 115. Write the numbers.

115, _____, _____, _____, _____, _____

Write the number.

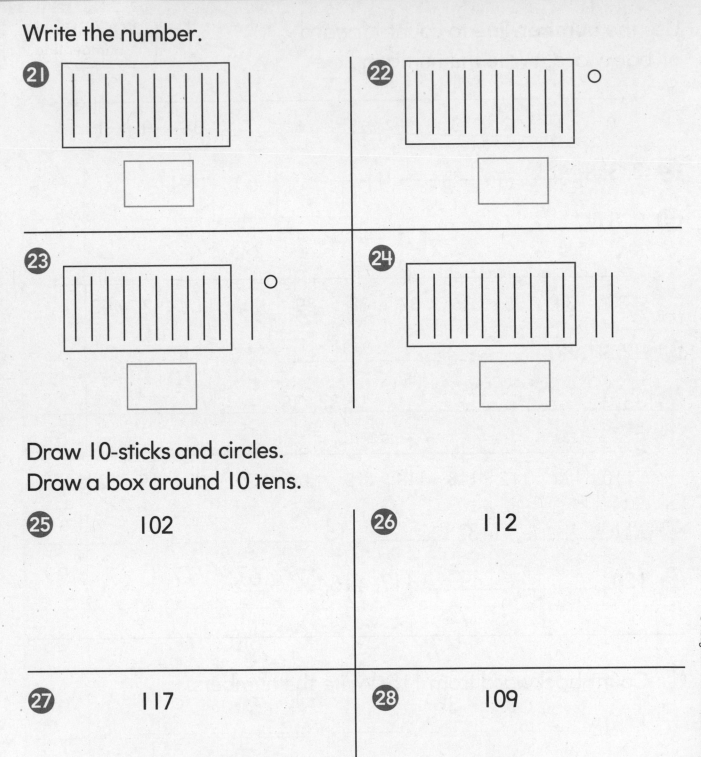

21

22

23

24

Draw 10-sticks and circles.
Draw a box around 10 tens.

25   102

26   112

27   117

28   109

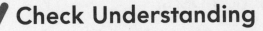 **Check Understanding**

How can you tell if 48 is 10 more or 10
less than 58?

Numbers Through 120

1 Listen to the directions.

1	11	21	31	41	51	61	71	81	91
2	12	22	32	42	52	62	72	82	92
3	13	23	33	43	53	63	73	83	93
4	14	24	34	44	54	64	74	84	94
5	15	25	35	45	55	65	75	85	95
6	16	26	36	46	56	66	76	86	96
7	17	27	37	47	57	67	77	87	97
8	18	28	38	48	58	68	78	88	98
9	19	29	39	49	59	69	79	89	99
10	20	30	40	50	60	70	80	90	100

Add tens.

2 89 + 10 = [ ]

3 43 + 20 = [ ]

4 28 + 50 = [ ]

5 32 + 40 = [ ]

6 11 + 20 = [ ]

7 42 + 30 = [ ]

8 52 + 40 = [ ]

9 12 + 40 = [ ]

10 27 + 60 = [ ]

11 61 + 30 = [ ]

Subtract tens.

12 30 − 20 = [ ]

13 60 − 10 = [ ]

14 70 − 40 = [ ]

15 70 − 20 = [ ]

16 90 − 60 = [ ]

17 80 − 70 = [ ]

18 90 − 10 = [ ]

19 50 − 40 = [ ]

20 20 − 10 = [ ]

21 40 − 10 = [ ]

Add and Subtract Tens and Number Patterns

Name _____

Write the number pattern rule.

22 5, 10, 15, 20, 25, 30   Rule: _____

23 10, 20, 30, 40, 50, 60   Rule: _____

24 33, 38, 43, 48, 53, 58   Rule: _____

25 22, 24, 26, 28, 30, 32   Rule: _____

Find the unknown numbers in the pattern.

26 46, 56, 66, _____, 86, _____

27 17, 19, 21, 23, _____, 27, 29, _____

Extend the number pattern.

28 62, 67, 72, 77, _____, _____, _____

29 34, 44, 54, 64, _____, _____, _____

30 47, 49, 51, 53, _____, _____, _____

31 12, 17, 22, 27, _____, _____, _____

32 Make a number pattern.
Use add 5 as the rule.

Look for the pattern. Write the rule and complete the table.

33 Maria runs every day for one week.   Rule: _____

Maria's Running Schedule

Day	Mon.	Tues.	Wed.	Thur.	Fri.	Sat.
Number of Minutes	12	17	22	27		

34 Choi reads every day for one week.   Rule: _____

Choi's Reading Schedule

Day	Mon.	Tues.	Wed.	Thur.	Fri.	Sat.
Number of Pages	11	13	15	17		

35 David practices every day for one week.   Rule: _____

David's Piano Practice Schedule

Day	Mon.	Tues.	Wed.	Thur.	Fri.	Sat.
Number of Minutes	16	21	26		36	

 Check Understanding

Write an equation to solve each problem.

Add 4 tens to 35.   Subtract 6 tens from 9 tens.

Add and Subtract Tens and Number Patterns

Name _____

Solve.

1 80 + 20 = ☐

2 30 + 70 = ☐

3 10 + ☐ = 100

4 50 + ☐ = 100

5 100 = 20 + ☐

6 100 = 40 + ☐

7 20 + 50 = ☐

8 10 + 80 = ☐

9 0 + 60 = ☐

10 20 + 20 = ☐

11 40 − 40 = ☐

12 80 − 0 = ☐

13 70 − 60 = ☐

14 60 − 30 = ☐

15 60 − 10 = ☐

10 + ☐ = 60

16 70 − 40 = ☐

40 + ☐ = 70

17 50 − 20 = ☐

20 + ☐ = 50

18 90 − 50 = ☐

50 + ☐ = 90

Add and Subtract Multiples of 10 **259**

19 Look at what Puzzled Penguin wrote.

$$70 - 20 = \boxed{5}$$

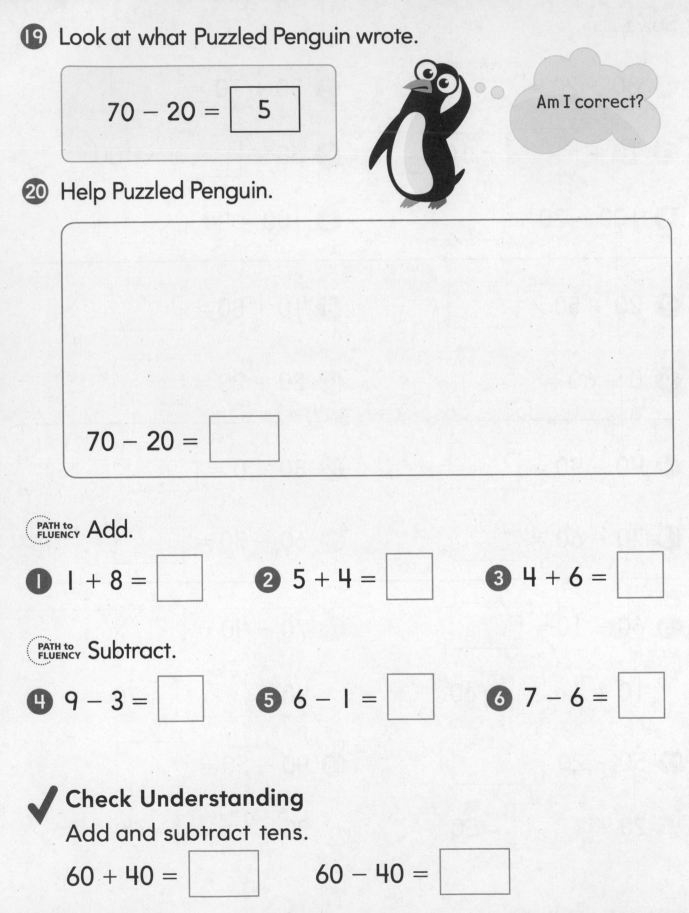

Am I correct?

20 Help Puzzled Penguin.

$$70 - 20 = \boxed{}$$

PATH to FLUENCY Add.

1 $1 + 8 = \boxed{}$ **2** $5 + 4 = \boxed{}$ **3** $4 + 6 = \boxed{}$

PATH to FLUENCY Subtract.

4 $9 - 3 = \boxed{}$ **5** $6 - 1 = \boxed{}$ **6** $7 - 6 = \boxed{}$

✔ **Check Understanding**

Add and subtract tens.

$$60 + 40 = \boxed{} \qquad 60 - 40 = \boxed{}$$

Add and Subtract Multiples of 10

Name _____

Use the picture.
Write the numbers to solve.

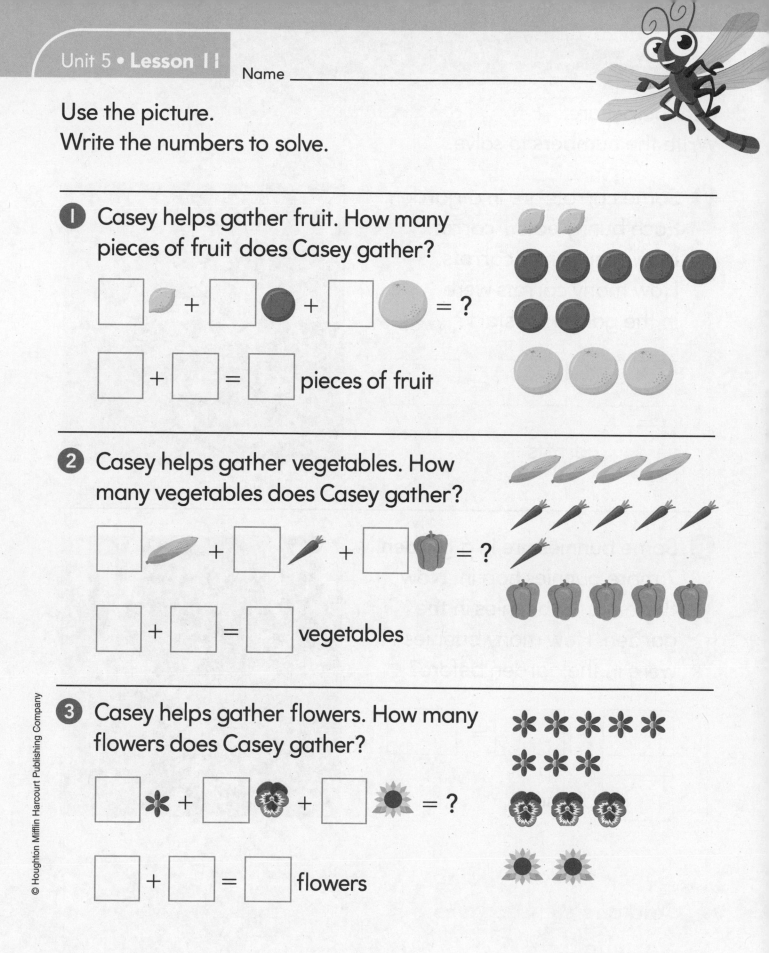

1 Casey helps gather fruit. How many
pieces of fruit does Casey gather?

☐ 🍋 + ☐ ● + ☐ 🍊 = ?

☐ + ☐ = ☐ pieces of fruit

2 Casey helps gather vegetables. How
many vegetables does Casey gather?

☐ 🌽 + ☐ 🥕 + ☐ 🫑 = ?

☐ + ☐ = ☐ vegetables

3 Casey helps gather flowers. How many
flowers does Casey gather?

☐ ✳ + ☐ 🌼 + ☐ 🌻 = ?

☐ + ☐ = ☐ flowers

Use the picture.
Write the numbers to solve.

 4 Some carrots are in a garden.
Each bunny eats 1 carrot.
Now there are 9 carrots.
How many carrots were
in the garden to start?

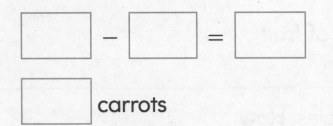

carrots

---

5 Some bunnies are in a garden.
7 more bunnies hop in. Now
there are 13 bunnies in the
garden. How many bunnies
were in the garden before?

bunnies

Focus on Problem Solving

Name _____   Date _____

Use the grid.

51	52	53	54	55	56	57	58	59	60
61	62	63	64	65	66	67	68	69	70
71	72	73	74	75	76	77	78	79	80

1 10 more than 54 is ☐ .

2 10 more than 68 is ☐ .

Add or subtract tens.

3 68 + 30 = ☐

4 52 + 20 = ☐

5 Find the unknown numbers in the pattern.

33, 35, 37, _____, 41, _____

Name _____ Date _____

Add.

1 3 + 3 = ☐   **2** 6 + 1 = ☐   **3** 4 + 2 = ☐

4 3 + 4 = ☐   **5** 6 + 2 = ☐   **6** 5 + 4 = ☐

Subtract.

7 6 − 4 = ☐   **8** 8 − 5 = ☐   **9** 7 − 3 = ☐

10 8 − 6 = ☐   **11** 9 − 2 = ☐   **12** 7 − 1 = ☐

13 10 − 10 = ☐   **14** 10 − 7 = ☐   **15** 9 − 8 = ☐

Name _____   Date _____

Match the box to the unknown partner.

1 $9 + \boxed{} = 15$ **2** $8 + \boxed{} = 15$ **3** $8 + \boxed{} = 17$

       •   •   •

       •   •   •

      9   6   7

Solve the story problem.

---

4 Beth has 16 bagels. She gives 8 to her friends. How many bagels does Beth have now?

$\boxed{}$ _____
      label

bagel

---

5 Meg has 6 books. Jen gives her some more books. Now Meg has 11 books. How many books does Jen give Meg?

$\boxed{}$ _____
      label

book

---

6 Luis has 7 blue pens, 4 red pens, and 3 green pens. How many pens does Luis have?

$\boxed{}$ _____
      label

pen

7 Is the sentence true? Choose Yes or No.

$14 - 8 = 5$ ○ Yes   ○ No

$16 - 7 = 9$ ○ Yes   ○ No

$17 - 9 = 8$ ○ Yes   ○ No

8 Start at 81. Count. Write the numbers through 110.

81	82	83							
91									

9 Draw a picture to solve the story problem.
Write a number sentence.
Answer the question.

There are 15 squirrels. Some are brown and
6 are gray. How many squirrels are brown?

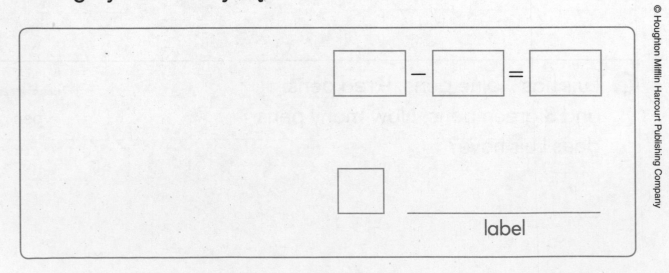

☐ − ☐ = ☐

☐ _____
          label

Solve.

10 57 + 20 = ☐   **11** 13 + 60 = ☐

12 80 − 40 = ☐   **13** 70 − 50 = ☐

14 80 + ☐ = 100   **15** 90 − ☐ = 70

Ring the number that makes the sentence true.

16 There are 9 red crayons, 3 green crayons, and 7 blue crayons in the box. How many crayons are in the box?

crayon

> 10
> 16   crayons are in the box.
> 19

---

17 Count backward from 118. Write the numbers.

118, _____, _____, _____, _____

---

18 Extend the number pattern.

53, 58, 63, 68, _____, _____, _____

19 There are 12 boys and girls on the bus.
How many boys and girls can there be?
Choose all possible answers.

- ○ 2 boys and 14 girls
- ○ 2 boys and 10 girls
- ○ 3 boys and 9 girls
- ○ 4 boys and 6 girls
- ○ 5 boys and 7 girls

---

20 Draw 20 to 30 more triangles.
Ring 10-groups. Count by tens and ones.
Write the numbers.

△ △ △ △ △ △ △ △ △ △

△ △ △ △ △ △ △ △ △ △

△ △ △ △ △ △ △ △ △ △

△ △ △ △ △ △ △ △ △ △

△ △ △ △ △ △

The number of triangles is ☐ .

10 less is ☐ . 10 more is ☐ .

Beach Day

Dan and Win look for shells at the beach.

1 **Part A**

Dan finds 32 shells. Draw to show 32 with tens and ones.

```
┌─────────────────────────────────────────┐
│                                         │
│                                         │
│                                         │
│                                         │
│                                         │
└─────────────────────────────────────────┘
```

Dan finds 20 more shells. How many shells does he have in all?

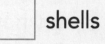 shells

Part B

Draw or tell how you know.

```
┌─────────────────────────────────────────┐
│                                         │
│                                         │
│                                         │
└─────────────────────────────────────────┘
```

2 **Part A**

Win finds 5 white shells, 3 brown shells, and 2 black shells. How many shells does she have in all?

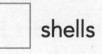 shells

Part B

Draw or write to tell how you know.

```
┌─────────────────────────────────────────┐
│                                         │
│                                         │
│                                         │
└─────────────────────────────────────────┘
```

3 **Part A**

Win finds 50 white shells, 30 brown shells, and 20 black shells. How many shells does she have in all?

☐ shells

Part B

Draw or tell how you know.

☐

Part C

Tell how adding 50, 30, and 20 is like adding 5, 3, and 2.

☐

4 **Part A**

At noon, Win had 50 white shells.
At 4 P.M., Win had 80 white shells.
How many shells did she find after noon?

☐ shells

Part B

Draw or tell how you know.

☐

Dear Family:

Children begin this unit by learning to organize, represent, and interpret data with two and three categories.

In the example below, children sort apples and bananas and represent the data using circles. They ask and answer questions about the data and learn to express comparative statements completely.

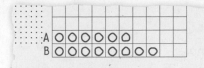

There are 2 more bananas than apples.

There are 2 fewer apples than bananas.

Later in the unit, children solve *Compare* story problems using comparison bars. Two examples are given below.

Jeremy has 10 crayons. Amanda has 3 crayons. How many more crayons does Jeremy have than Amanda?

Abby has 8 erasers. Ramon has 6 more erasers than Abby has. How many erasers does Ramon have?

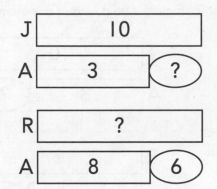

While working on homework, ask your child to explain to you how to use comparison bars to solve these types of story problems.
If you have any questions, please do not hesitate to contact me.

Sincerely,
Your child's teacher

Estimada familia:

Al comenzar esta unidad, los niños aprenderán a organizar, representar e interpretar datos de dos y tres categorías.

En el ejemplo de abajo, los niños clasifican manzanas y plátanos, y representan los datos usando círculos. Formulan y responden preguntas acerca de los datos y aprenden cómo expresar enunciados comparativos completos.

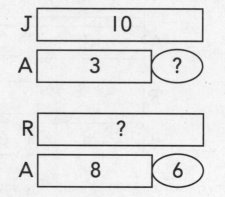

Hay 2 plátanos más que manzanas.

Hay 2 manzanas menos que plátanos.

Más adelante en la unidad, los niños resolverán problemas que requieran *comparar*, usando barras de comparación. Abajo se dan dos ejemplos.

Jeremy tiene 10 crayones.
Amanda tiene 3 crayones.
¿Cuántos crayones más que
Amanda tiene Jeremy?

Abby tiene 8 borradores.
Ramón tiene 6 borradores
más que Abby. ¿Cuántos
borradores tiene Ramón?

Mientras hace la tarea, pida a su niño que le explique cómo usar las barras de comparación para resolver este tipo de problemas.

Si tiene alguna pregunta, no dude en comunicarse conmigo.

Atentamente,
El maestro de su niño

© Houghton Mifflin Harcourt Publishing Company

Explore Representing Data

bar graph	fewest
data	more
fewer	most

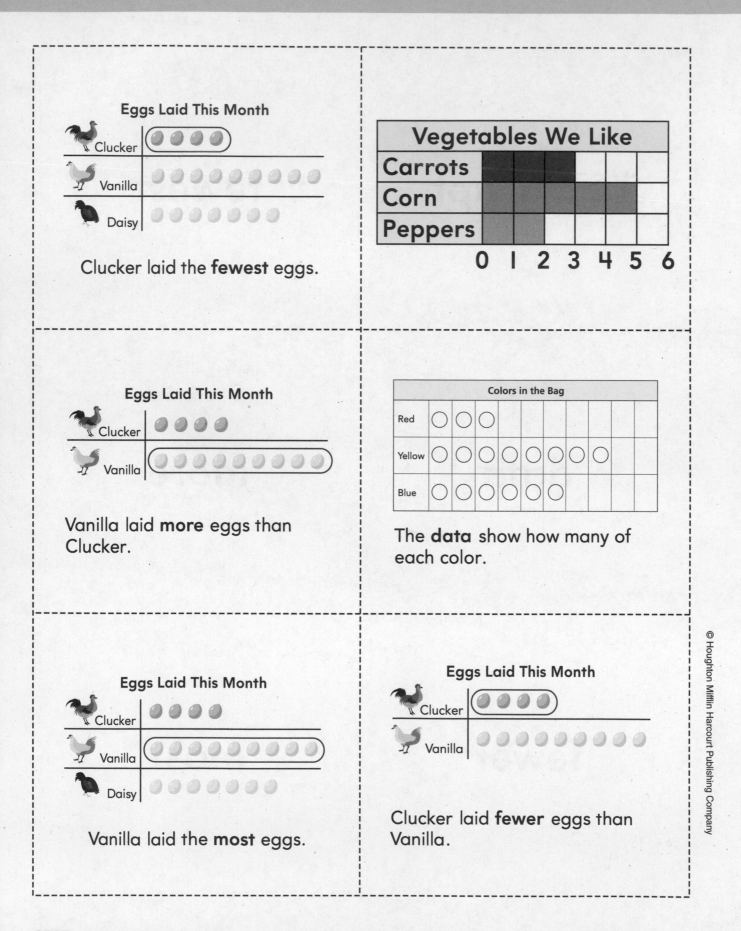

Eggs Laid This Month

Clucker
Vanilla
Daisy

Clucker laid the **fewest** eggs.

Vegetables We Like						
Carrots						
Corn						
Peppers						
0	1	2	3	4	5	6

Eggs Laid This Month

Clucker
Vanilla

Vanilla laid **more** eggs than Clucker.

Colors in the Bag								
Red	○	○	○					
Yellow	○	○	○	○	○	○	○	○
Blue	○	○	○	○	○	○		

The **data** show how many of each color.

Eggs Laid This Month

Clucker
Vanilla
Daisy

Vanilla laid the **most** eggs.

Eggs Laid This Month

Clucker
Vanilla

Clucker laid **fewer** eggs than Vanilla.

sort

tally mark

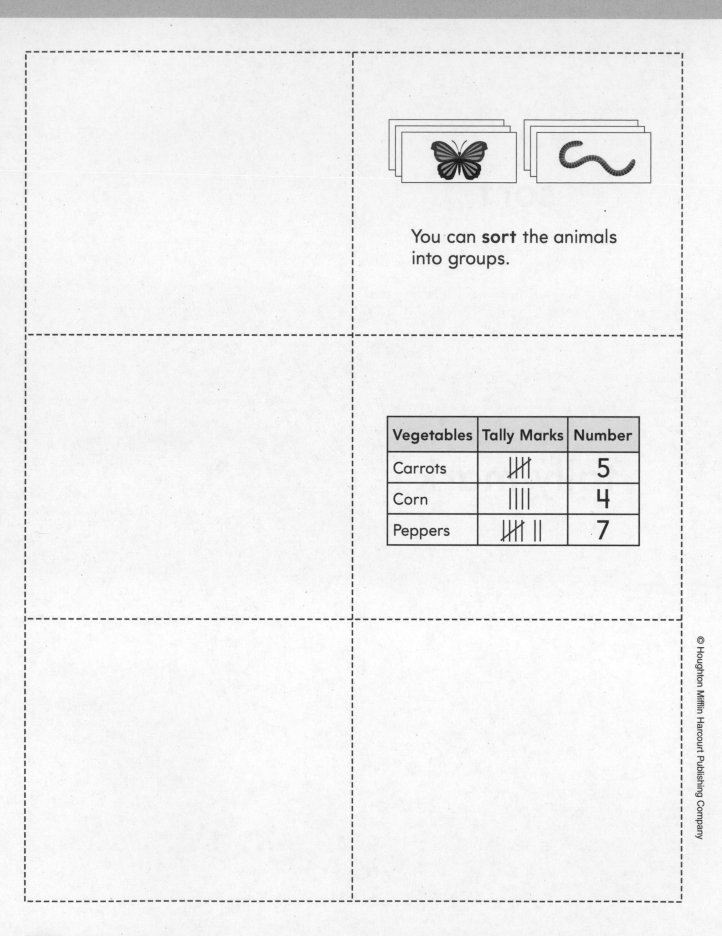

You can **sort** the animals into groups.

Vegetables	Tally Marks	Number
Carrots	|||||	5
Corn	||||	4
Peppers	||||| ||	7

Name _____

Cut out the cards.
Which animals have legs?
Which animals do not have legs?
Sort the animals.

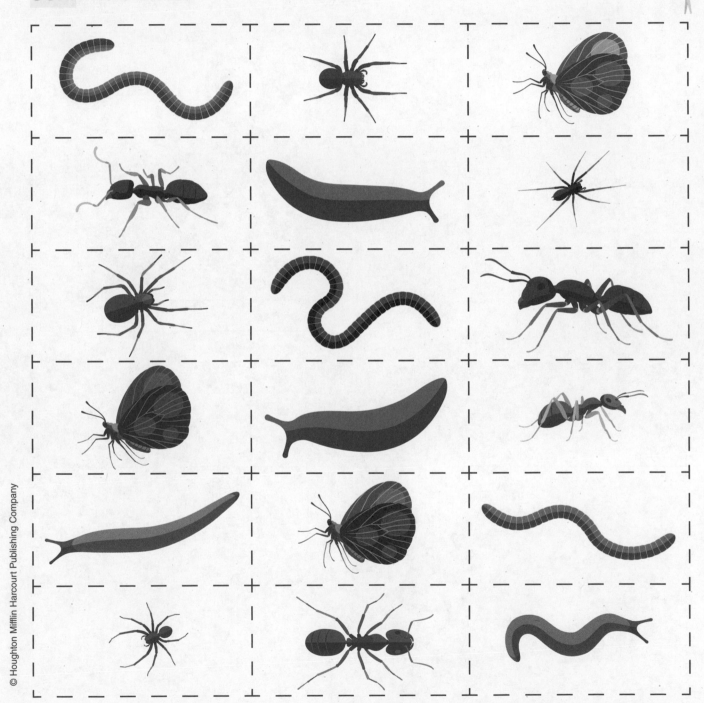

Explore Representing Data

Name _____

1 Use circles and 5-groups to record.
Write how many in each group.

VOCABULARY
data
more
fewer

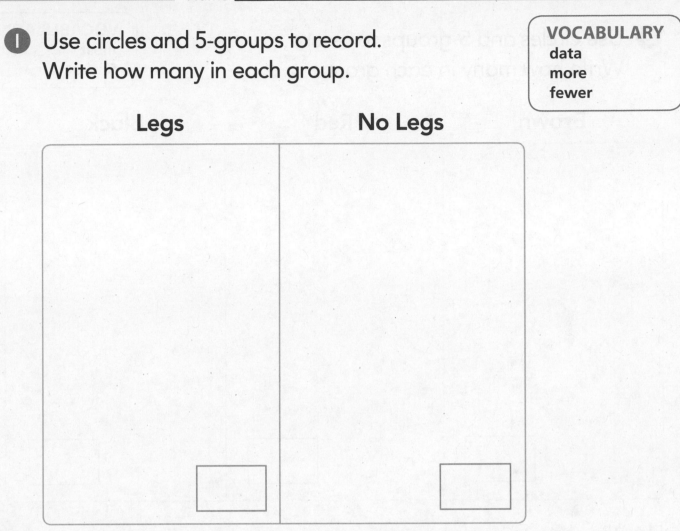

Legs   No Legs

Use the **data** to complete.

2 How many animals in all? _____

3 Ring the group with **more** animals.

4 Cross out the group with **fewer** animals.

5 Use circles and 5-groups to record.
Write how many in each group.

VOCABULARY
most
fewest

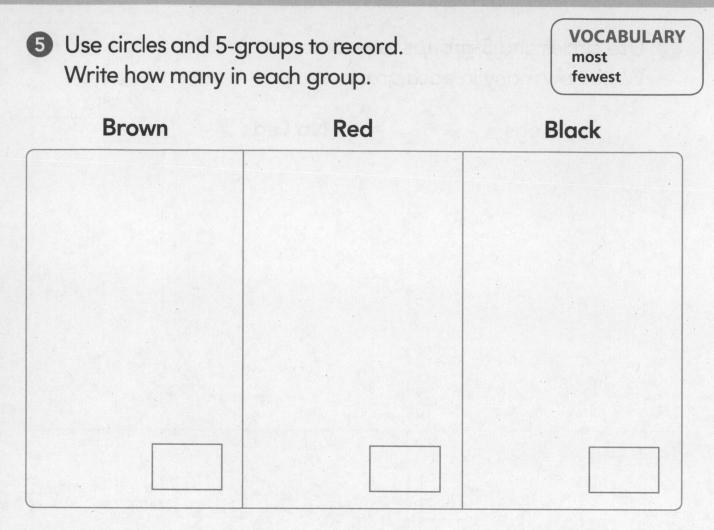

| Brown | Red | Black |

Use the data to complete.

6 How many animals in all? _____

7 Ring the group with the **most** animals.

8 Cross out the group with the **fewest** animals.

✔ **Check Understanding**

Draw circles and 5-groups to show 9 black
animals and 8 green animals.

black animals:

green animals:

Explore Representing Data

Name _____

1 Draw matching lines to compare.
Complete the sentences.
Ring the word **more** or **fewer**.

Mara

Todd

Mara has [ ] **more fewer** apples than Todd.

Todd has [ ] **more fewer** apples than Mara.

---

2 Each ant gets 1 crumb.
How many more crumbs are needed? [ ]

3 Draw circles for the crumbs.

Crumbs

Ants

---

4 Each bee gets 1 flower.
How many extra flowers are there? [ ]

5 Ring the extra flowers.

Flowers

Bees

6 Sort the fruit. Record with pictures.
Write how many in each group.

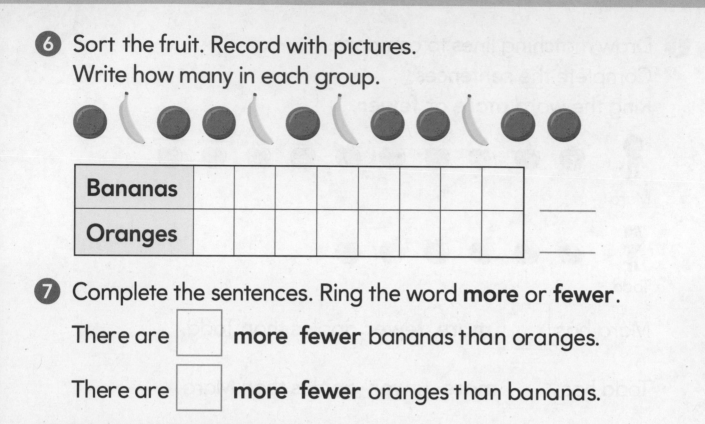

Bananas									____
Oranges									____

7 Complete the sentences. Ring the word **more** or **fewer**.

There are ☐ **more fewer** bananas than oranges.

There are ☐ **more fewer** oranges than bananas.

---

8 Sort the vegetables. Record with circles.
Write how many in each group.

Carrots										____
Peppers										____

9 Complete the sentence. Ring the word **more** or **fewer**.

There are ☐ **more fewer** peppers than carrots.

✓ **Check Understanding**

Represent 5 apples and 9 bananas. How many more bananas are there? How many fewer apples are there?

Organize Categorical Data

Name _____

1 Look at what Puzzled Penguin wrote.

Am I correct?

Stripes	O	O	O	O	O	O	O	O	O
Spots	O	O	O	O	O				

There are 4 more fish with stripes than with spots.

There are 4 fewer fish with spots than with stripes.

2 Help Puzzled Penguin.

Stripes									
Spots									

There are ☐ more fish with stripes than with spots.

There are ☐ fewer fish with spots than with stripes.

Use Stair Steps to Represent Data **279**

3 Sort the animals. Record with circles.
Write how many in each group.

Dogs									
Cats									

_____

_____

4 Complete the sentence. Ring the word **more** or **fewer**.

There are ⬜ **more** **fewer** dogs than cats.

PATH to FLUENCY Add.

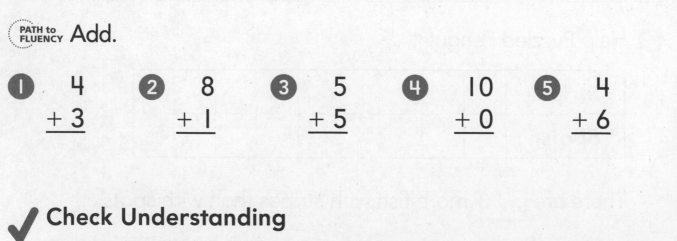

1 $\begin{array}{r} 4 \\ +3 \\ \hline \end{array}$ **2** $\begin{array}{r} 8 \\ +1 \\ \hline \end{array}$ **3** $\begin{array}{r} 5 \\ +5 \\ \hline \end{array}$ **4** $\begin{array}{r} 10 \\ +0 \\ \hline \end{array}$ **5** $\begin{array}{r} 4 \\ +6 \\ \hline \end{array}$

✔ **Check Understanding**
Draw Stair Steps to compare 9 and 5.

Use Stair Steps to Represent Data

1 Discuss the data.

2 Write how many in each category.

Eggs Laid This Month

🐓 Clucker	🥚🥚🥚🥚	___
🐔 Daisy	🥚🥚🥚🥚🥚🥚🥚🥚🥚	___
🐔 Vanilla	🥚🥚🥚🥚🥚🥚🥚	___

Animals in the Pond

Frogs		___
Fish		___
Ducks		___

Hot Dogs Sold at the Fair

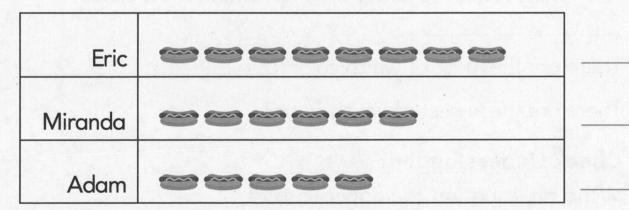

Eric		___
Miranda		___
Adam		___

Watch as each cube is taken from the bag.

3 Draw squares to show how many of each color.

Colors in the Bag										
Red										
Yellow										
Blue										

Use the data to answer the questions.

4 How many red cubes are in the bag? _____

5 How many yellow cubes are in the bag?

_____

6 How many blue cubes are in the bag? _____

7 How many more blue cubes are there than red cubes?

_____

8 How many fewer red cubes are there than yellow cubes?

_____

9 There are the most of which color? _____

10 There are the fewest of which color? _____

✔ **Check Understanding**
Write an equation to show the total
number of cubes in the bag.

Data Sets with Three Categories

Name _____

Use the data to answer the questions.

Favorite Vegetable

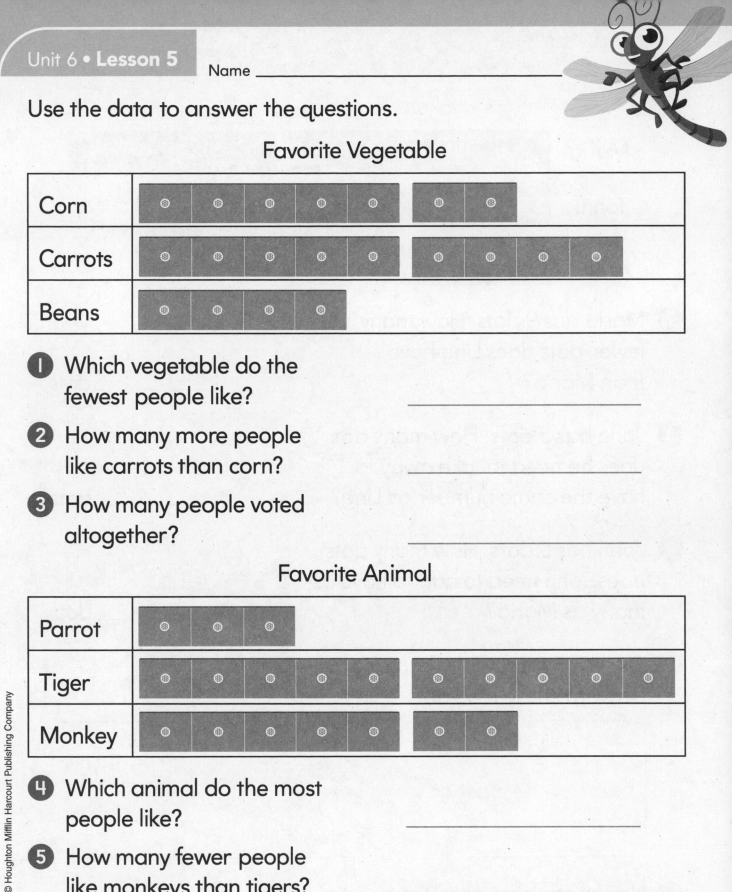

Corn	⊙ ⊙ ⊙ ⊙ ⊙ ⊙ ⊙
Carrots	⊙ ⊙ ⊙ ⊙ ⊙ ⊙ ⊙ ⊙ ⊙
Beans	⊙ ⊙ ⊙ ⊙

1 Which vegetable do the
fewest people like? _____

2 How many more people
like carrots than corn? _____

3 How many people voted
altogether? _____

Favorite Animal

Parrot	⊙ ⊙ ⊙
Tiger	⊙ ⊙ ⊙ ⊙ ⊙ ⊙ ⊙ ⊙ ⊙
Monkey	⊙ ⊙ ⊙ ⊙ ⊙ ⊙ ⊙

4 Which animal do the most
people like? _____

5 How many fewer people
like monkeys than tigers? _____

6 How many people like
parrots best? _____

Solve.

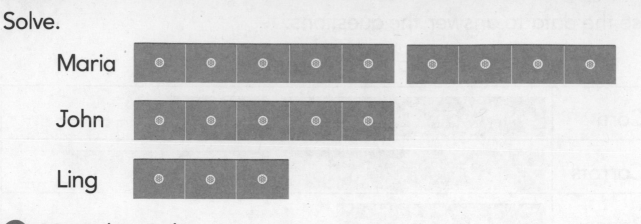

Maria

John

Ling

7 Maria has 9 dots. How many fewer dots does Ling have than Maria?

_____ dots

8 John has 5 dots. How many dots does he need to take away to have the same number as Ling?

_____ dots

9 John has 5 dots. How many dots does John need to add to have as many as Maria?

_____ dots

10 Teo has 5 more dots than Ling. Draw to show Teo's dots.

11 How many dots does Teo need to add to have the same number as Maria?

_____

Data Collecting

Name _____

12 Sort the vegetables. Record with **tally marks**.
Make a **bar graph**.

VOCABULARY
tally mark
bar graph

Vegetables	Tally Marks	Number
Carrots		
Corn		
Peppers		

Number of Vegetables

Carrots									
Corn									
Peppers									

0   1   2   3   4   5   6   7   8   9

Use the data to answer the questions.

13 How many more carrots are there than ears of corn?

_____

14 How many more peppers are there than carrots?

_____

15 How many fewer ears of corn are there than peppers?

_____

16 Sort the balls. Record with tally marks.
Make a bar graph.

Balls	Tally Marks	Number
Baseballs		
Basketballs		
Soccer balls		

Number of Balls

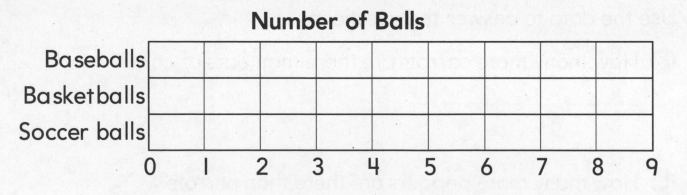

✓ **Check Understanding**

Draw 3 Stair Steps of different lengths.
Use the terms more, fewer, most,
and fewest to compare the dots.

Data Collecting

Name _____   Date _____

1 Write how many in each group.

Use the data to complete each sentence.

2 There are ☐ more pencils than markers.

3 There are ☐ more crayons than pencils.

4 There are ☐ fewer markers than crayons.

5 There are ☐ fewer pencils than crayons.

Name _____   Date _____

Add.

1 $\begin{array}{r} 1 \\ +2 \\ \hline \end{array}$

2 $\begin{array}{r} 3 \\ +1 \\ \hline \end{array}$

3 $\begin{array}{r} 2 \\ +3 \\ \hline \end{array}$

4 $\begin{array}{r} 2 \\ +4 \\ \hline \end{array}$

5 $\begin{array}{r} 4 \\ +3 \\ \hline \end{array}$

6 $\begin{array}{r} 6 \\ +1 \\ \hline \end{array}$

7 $\begin{array}{r} 4 \\ +4 \\ \hline \end{array}$

8 $\begin{array}{r} 5 \\ +2 \\ \hline \end{array}$

9 $\begin{array}{r} 4 \\ +5 \\ \hline \end{array}$

10 $\begin{array}{r} 6 \\ +3 \\ \hline \end{array}$

11 $\begin{array}{r} 5 \\ +3 \\ \hline \end{array}$

12 $\begin{array}{r} 8 \\ +2 \\ \hline \end{array}$

13 $\begin{array}{r} 6 \\ +2 \\ \hline \end{array}$

14 $\begin{array}{r} 5 \\ +5 \\ \hline \end{array}$

15 $\begin{array}{r} 2 \\ +7 \\ \hline \end{array}$

Name _____

Solve the story problem.
Use comparison bars.

Show your work.

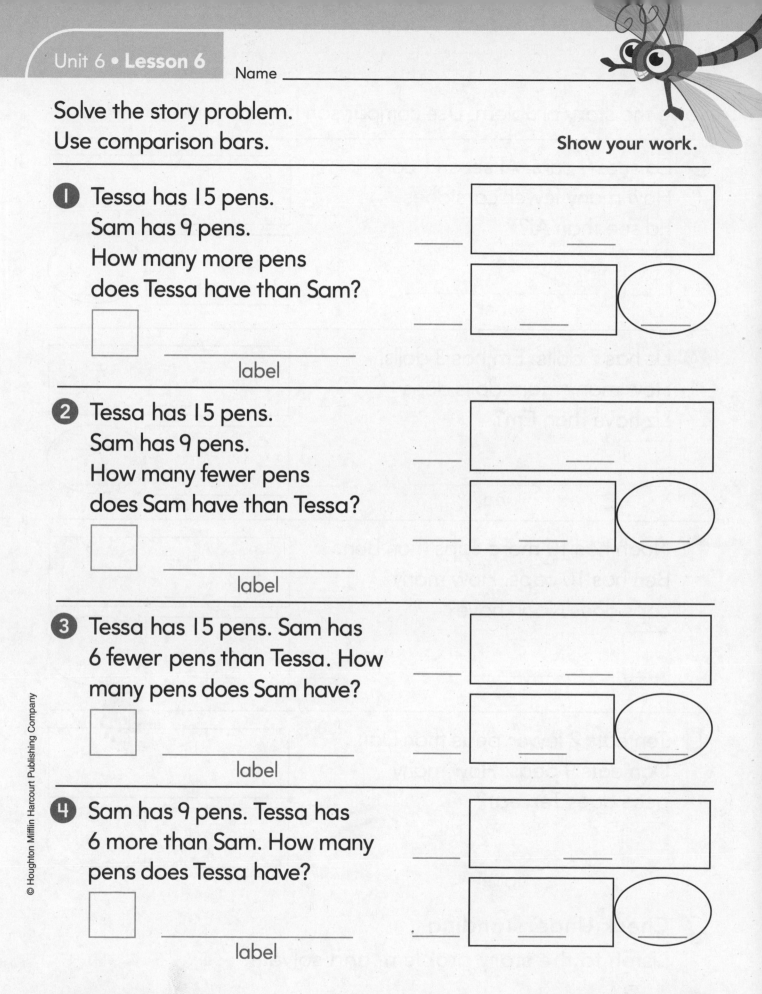

1 Tessa has 15 pens.
Sam has 9 pens.
How many more pens
does Tessa have than Sam?

☐ _____
label

2 Tessa has 15 pens.
Sam has 9 pens.
How many fewer pens
does Sam have than Tessa?

☐ _____
label

3 Tessa has 15 pens. Sam has
6 fewer pens than Tessa. How
many pens does Sam have?

☐ _____
label

4 Sam has 9 pens. Tessa has
6 more than Sam. How many
pens does Tessa have?

☐ _____
label

Introduce Comparison Bars **289**

Solve the story problem. Use comparison bars.   **Show your work.**

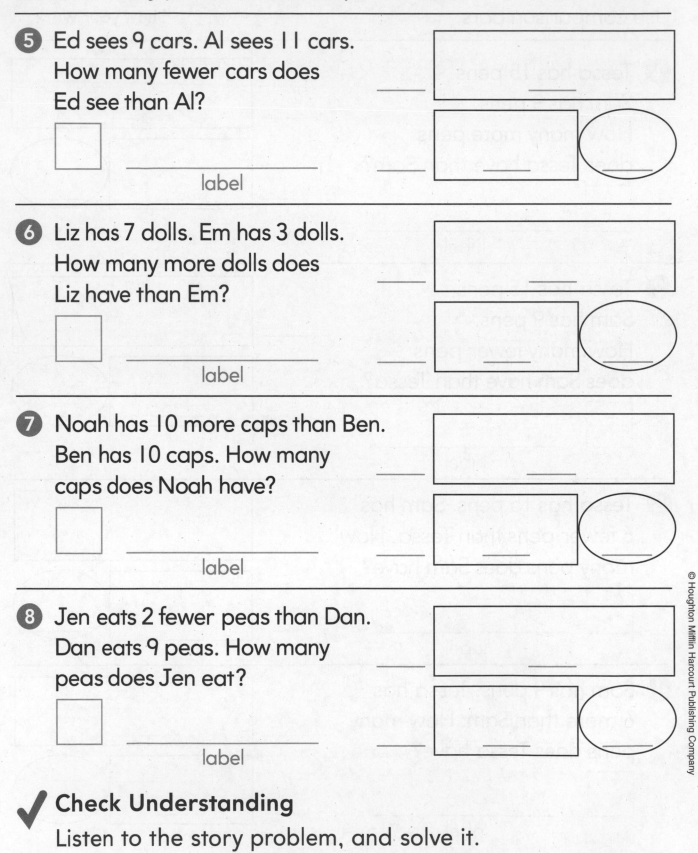

5 Ed sees 9 cars. Al sees 11 cars.
How many fewer cars does
Ed see than Al?

[ ] _____
         label

6 Liz has 7 dolls. Em has 3 dolls.
How many more dolls does
Liz have than Em?

[ ] _____
         label

7 Noah has 10 more caps than Ben.
Ben has 10 caps. How many
caps does Noah have?

[ ] _____
         label

8 Jen eats 2 fewer peas than Dan.
Dan eats 9 peas. How many
peas does Jen eat?

[ ] _____
         label

✔ **Check Understanding**
Listen to the story problem, and solve it.

Introduce Comparison Bars

Name _____

Solve and discuss.

1 There are 14 tigers and 8 bears. How many more tigers than bears are there?

☐ _____
     label

$14 = 8 +$ ☐

$14 - 8 =$ ☐

T | 14

B | 8 | ◯

14 / \ 8 ☐

2 There are 12 lions. There are 5 fewer camels than lions. How many camels are there?

☐ _____
     label

$5 +$ ☐ $= 12$

$12 - 5 =$ ☐

L | 12

C | ☐ | 5 ◯

12 / \ ☐ 5

3 There are 7 elephants. There are 6 more zebras than elephants. How many zebras are there?

☐ _____
     label

$7 + 6 =$ ☐

Z | ☐

E | 7 | 6 ◯

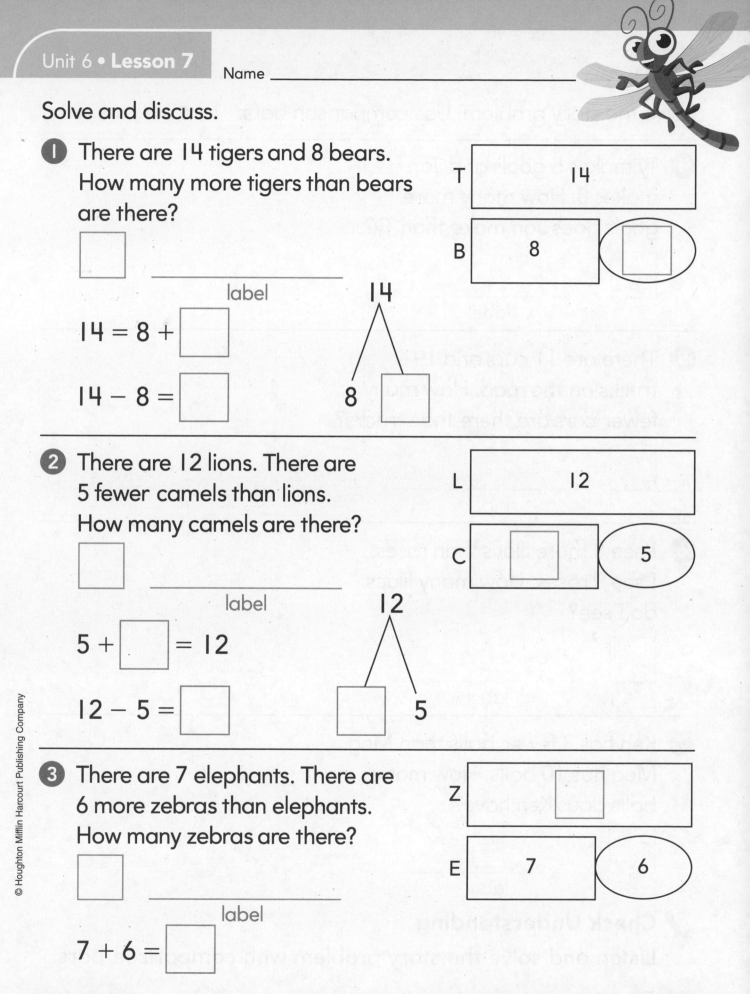

Solve the story problem. Use comparison bars.   **Show your work.**

4 Ty makes 5 goals and Jon
makes 8. How many more
goals does Jon make than Ty?

☐ _____
         label

5 There are 11 cars and 19
trucks on the road. How many
fewer cars are there than trucks?

☐ _____
         label

6 I see 8 more lilacs than roses.
I see 9 roses. How many lilacs
do I see?

☐ _____
         label

7 Ken has 3 fewer balls than Meg.
Meg has 10 balls. How many
balls does Ken have?

☐ _____
         label

✓ **Check Understanding**
Listen and solve the story problem with comparison bars.

Comparison Bars and Comparing Language

Solve the story problem.
Use comparison bars.

Show your work.

1 Cory's cat has 11 kittens.
Eva's cat has 3 kittens.
How many fewer kittens does
Eva's cat have than Cory's?

◻ _____
label

2 There were 3 bicycles here
yesterday. There are 7 more
bicycles here today. How many
bicycles are here today?

◻ _____
label

3 Ms. Perez has 15 horses.
Mr. Drew has 9 horses.
How many more horses does
Ms. Perez have than Mr. Drew?

◻ _____
label

Solve *Compare* Problems **293**

Solve the story problem. Use comparison bars.   **Show your work.**

4 Jim pops 5 fewer balloons than Sadie. Jim pops 9 balloons. How many balloons does Sadie pop?

☐ _____
　　　 label

5 Nick hikes 12 miles in the forest. Nick hikes 4 more miles than Zia. How many miles does Zia hike?

☐ _____
　　　 label

PATH to FLUENCY Subtract.

1 $\begin{array}{r} 9 \\ -1 \\ \hline \end{array}$ **2** $\begin{array}{r} 6 \\ -3 \\ \hline \end{array}$ **3** $\begin{array}{r} 8 \\ -6 \\ \hline \end{array}$ **4** $\begin{array}{r} 5 \\ -5 \\ \hline \end{array}$ **5** $\begin{array}{r} 9 \\ -7 \\ \hline \end{array}$

6 $\begin{array}{r} 4 \\ -2 \\ \hline \end{array}$ **7** $\begin{array}{r} 10 \\ -6 \\ \hline \end{array}$ **8** $\begin{array}{r} 9 \\ -3 \\ \hline \end{array}$ **9** $\begin{array}{r} 7 \\ -5 \\ \hline \end{array}$ **10** $\begin{array}{r} 6 \\ -1 \\ \hline \end{array}$

 Check Understanding
Listen to the story problem, and use comparison bars and an equation to solve.

Solve *Compare* Problems

Name _____

Liam collects data at the park. He wants to know how many animals can fly and how many animals cannot fly.

1 Sort the animals.
Record with circles and 5-groups.

Animals That Can Fly	Animals That Cannot Fly

Use the data to complete.

2 How many animals can fly? _____

3 How many animals cannot fly? _____

4 How many animals does Liam see in all?

_____

5 How many more animals can fly than cannot fly?

_____

Solve.
Show your work.

6 There are 8 swings.
12 children want to swing.
How many children must
wait to swing?

☐ _____
label

7 10 bikes are on the rack.
7 children start to ride. How
many bikes do not have a rider?

☐ _____
label

Solve the story problem.
Use comparison bars.

Show your work.

1 Keith scores 10 points. Eric scores 7 points. How many fewer points does Eric score than Keith?

K

E

_____
label

2 There are 2 more white rabbits than brown rabbits. There are 9 brown rabbits. How many white rabbits are there?

W

B

_____
label

3 Don eats 6 more grapes than Meg. Meg eats 12 grapes. How many grapes does Don eat?

D

M

_____
label

Name _____ Date _____

Subtract.

1   4
     − 2

2   5
     − 1

3   3
     − 3

4   6
     − 5

5   7
     − 4

6   6
     − 3

7   8
     − 3

8   8
     − 8

9   7
     − 2

10   9
      − 6

11   8
      − 5

12   9
      − 4

13   10
      − 3

14   10
      − 8

15   9
      − 3

1 Sort the animals. Record with circles.

2 Write how many in each group.

Stripes										
Spots										
Solid										

Use the data. Choose the answer.

3 How many fewer solid-color animals
are there than animals with stripes?

○ 4   ○ 6   ○ 7

4 How many animals are there in all?

○ 9   ○ 16   ○ 19

5 Sort the fruit. Record with circles.
Write how many in each group.

Apples								
Bananas								
Oranges								

6 Is the sentence true? Choose Yes or No.

There are more oranges than bananas. ○ Yes ○ No
There are more apples than oranges. ○ Yes ○ No
There are fewer bananas than apples. ○ Yes ○ No

7 How many fewer oranges are there than apples?

8 How many more bananas are there than oranges?

9 How many pieces of fruit are there in all?

_____
label

Solve the story problem.
Use comparison bars.

10 Rico sees 5 more cats than dogs.
He sees 7 dogs.
How many cats does he see?

☐ _____
  label

11 Nori has 15 coins.
Maria has 6 coins.
How many more coins does
Nori have than Maria?

☐ _____
  label

Ring the answer. Use comparison bars.

12 Kim picks 13 tulips.
Emily picks 8 tulips.
How many fewer tulips does
Emily pick than Kim?

Emily picks | 5 | fewer tulips than Kim.
            | 8 |
            | 13 |

13 A class is going on a field trip. They collect data about places to go. Each child votes. The teacher draws one circle for each vote.

Field Trip Ideas

Park	Zoo	Museum
ooooo	ooooo ooooo	oooo

Write two questions about the data.
Answer each question.

_____

- - - - - - - - - - - - - - - - - - - -

_____

- - - - - - - - - - - - - - - - - - - -

_____

- - - - - - - - - - - - - - - - - - - -

_____

- - - - - - - - - - - - - - - - - - - -

_____

- - - - - - - - - - - - - - - - - - - -

_____

- - - - - - - - - - - - - - - - - - - -

Sort and Compare

Use all 20 strips of paper for this activity.

 Part A Sort the strips. Draw 5-groups and circles in the table to show how many strips you have of each color.

My Color Strips		
Red	**Blue**	**Yellow**

Part B How many strips are **not** blue?

☐ not blue

Draw or tell how you know.

```
```

2 **Part A** How many more strips are there of the color with the most strips than the color with the

fewest strips? ☐

Part B Draw or tell how you know.

```
```

Compare Animals

Use the data to answer the questions.

Frogs	⬤	⬤	⬤	⬤					
Bunnies	⬤	⬤	⬤	⬤	⬤	⬤	⬤	⬤	⬤
Deer	⬤	⬤	⬤	⬤	⬤	⬤	⬤		

3 **Part A** There are ☐ frogs.

There are ☐ fewer frogs than deer.

How many frogs and bunnies are there?

☐ frogs and bunnies

Part B How many more bunnies are there than deer?

☐ more bunnies

Draw or tell how you know.

4 **Part A** How many animals are there in all?

☐ animals

Part B Draw or tell how you know.

Dear Family:

Your child has begun a unit that focuses on measurement and geometry. Children will begin the unit by learning to tell and write time in hours and half-hours on an analog and digital clock.

hour : minute

Later in the unit, children will work with both 2-dimensional and 3-dimensional shapes.

They will learn to distinguish between defining and non-defining attributes of shapes. For example, rectangles have four sides and four square corners. A square is a special kind of rectangle with all sides the same length. The shapes below are different sizes, colors, and orientations, but they are all rectangles.

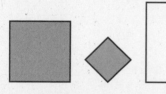

Later in the unit, children will compose shapes to create new shapes.

 A cone and a rectangular prism were used to make this new shape.

Children will also learn to partition circles and rectangles into two and four equal shares. They describe the shares using the words *halves*, *fourths*, and *quarters*.

 This circle is partitioned into halves.

 This circle is partitioned into fourths or quarters.

Children generalize that partitioning a shape into more equal shares creates smaller shares: one fourth of the circle above is smaller than one half of the circle.

Another concept in this unit is length measurement. Children order three objects by length.

These objects are in order from longest to shortest.

They also use same-size length units such as paper clips to measure the length of an object.

This ribbon is 4 paper clips long.

You can help your child practice these new skills at home. If you have any questions, please contact me.

Sincerely,
Your child's teacher

Estimada familia:

Su niño ha comenzado una unidad sobre medidas y geometría. Comenzará esta unidad aprendiendo a leer y escribir la hora en punto y la media hora en un reloj analógico y en uno digital.

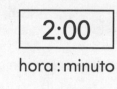

hora : minuto

Después, trabajará con figuras bidimensionales y tridimensionales.

Aprenderá a distinguir entre atributos que definen a una figura y los que no la definen. Por ejemplo, los rectángulos tienen cuatro lados y cuatro esquinas. Un cuadrado es un tipo especial de rectángulo que tiene lados de igual longitud. Las figuras de abajo tienen diferente tamaño, color y orientación, pero todas son rectángulos.

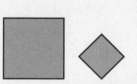 

Más adelante en la unidad, los niños acomodarán figuras de diferentes maneras para formar nuevas figuras.

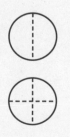 Para formar esta nueva figura se usaron un cono y un prisma rectangular.

También aprenderán a dividir círculos y rectángulos en dos y cuatro partes iguales. Describirán esas partes usando *mitades* y *cuartos*.

 Este círculo está dividido en mitades.

Este círculo está dividido en cuartos.

Deducirán que si dividen un figura en más partes iguales, obtendrán partes más pequeñas: un cuarto del círculo es más pequeño que una mitad.

Otro concepto que se enseña en esta unidad es la medición de longitudes. Los niños ordenan tres objetos según su longitud.

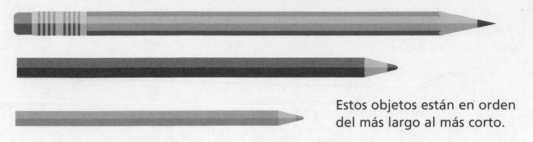

Estos objetos están en orden del más largo al más corto.

También usan unidades de la misma longitud, tales como clips, para medir la longitud de un objeto.

Esta cinta mide 4 clips de longitud.

Usted puede ayudar a su niño a practicar estas nuevas destrezas en casa. Si tiene alguna pregunta, comuníquese conmigo.

Atentamente,
El maestro de su niño

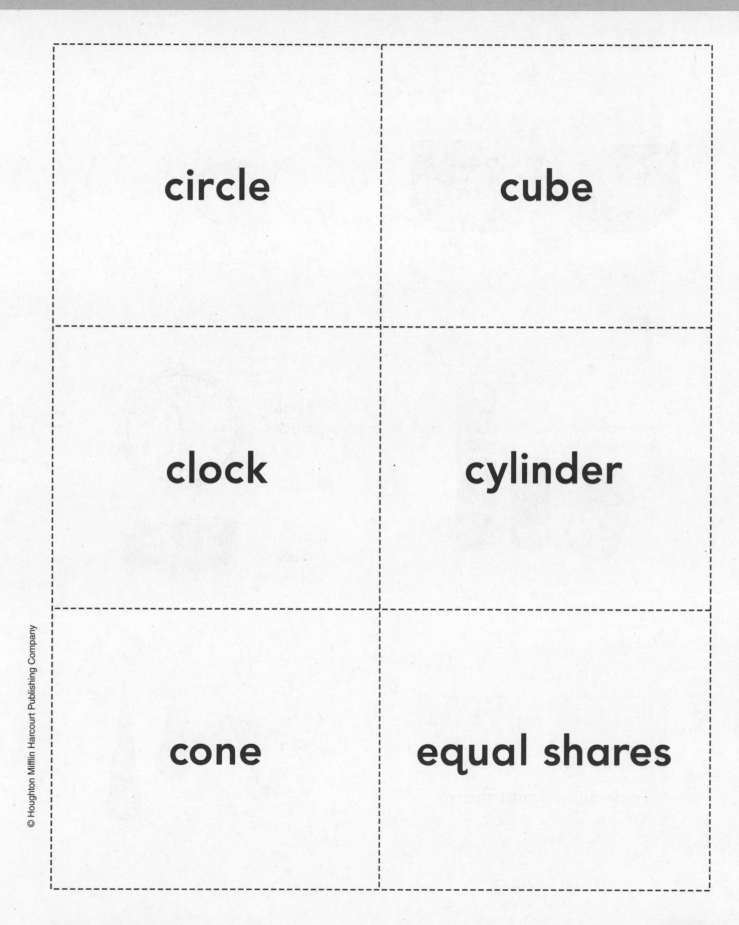

circle	cube
clock	cylinder
cone	equal shares

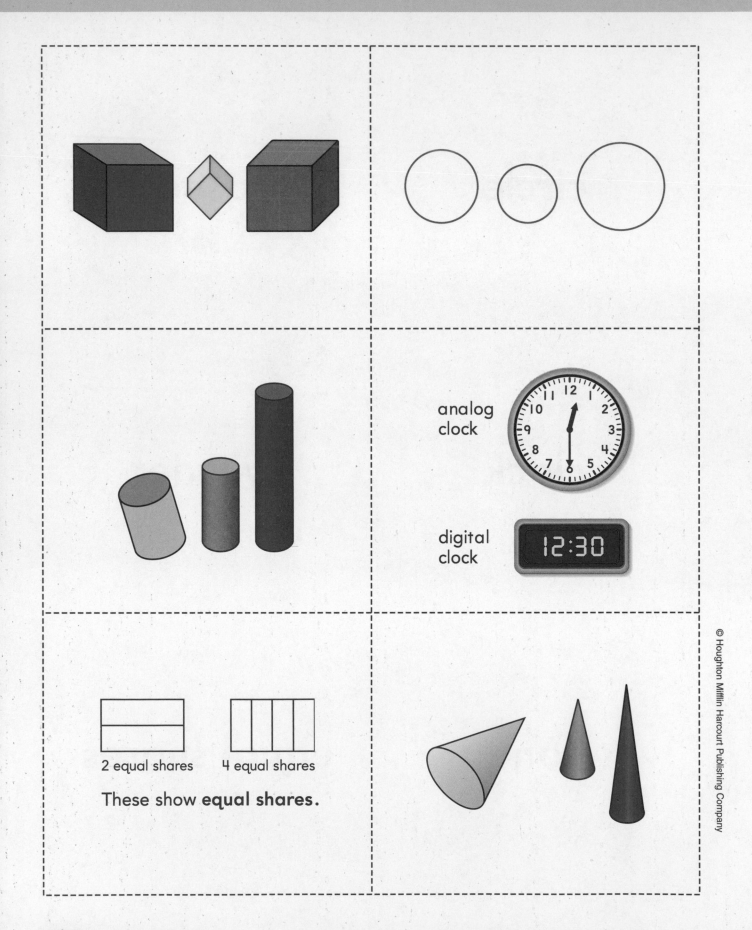

analog
clock

digital
clock

12:30

2 equal shares   4 equal shares

These show **equal shares**.

fourth of	half of
fourths	halves
half-hour	hour hand

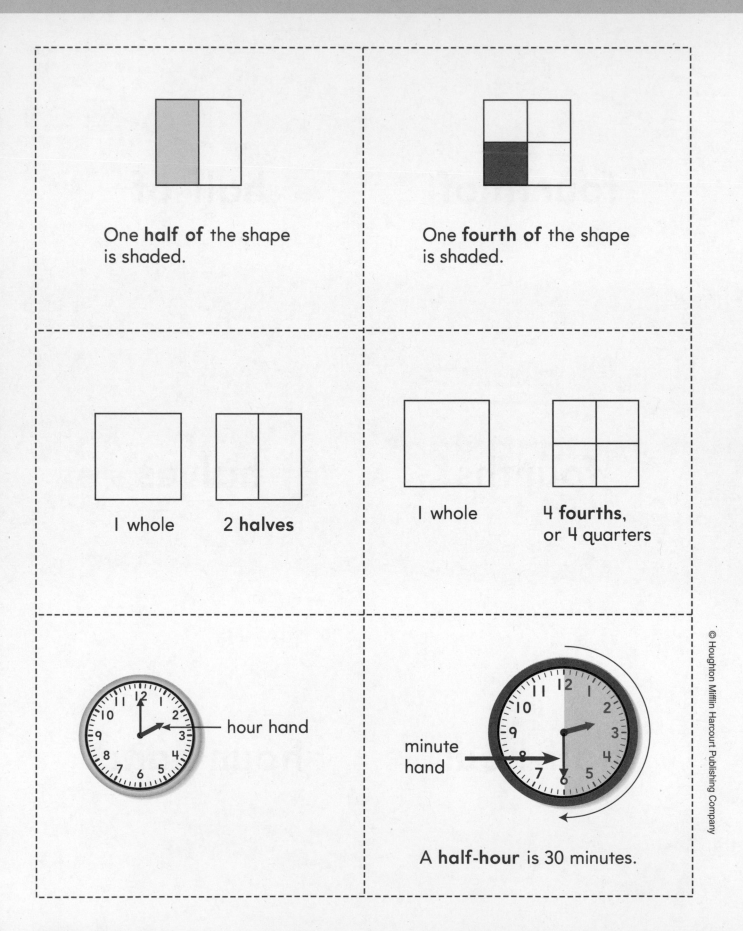

One **half of** the shape is shaded.

One **fourth of** the shape is shaded.

1 whole   2 **halves**

1 whole   4 **fourths,** or 4 quarters

hour hand

minute hand

A **half-hour** is 30 minutes.

rectangle

sphere

rectangular prism

square corner

side

square

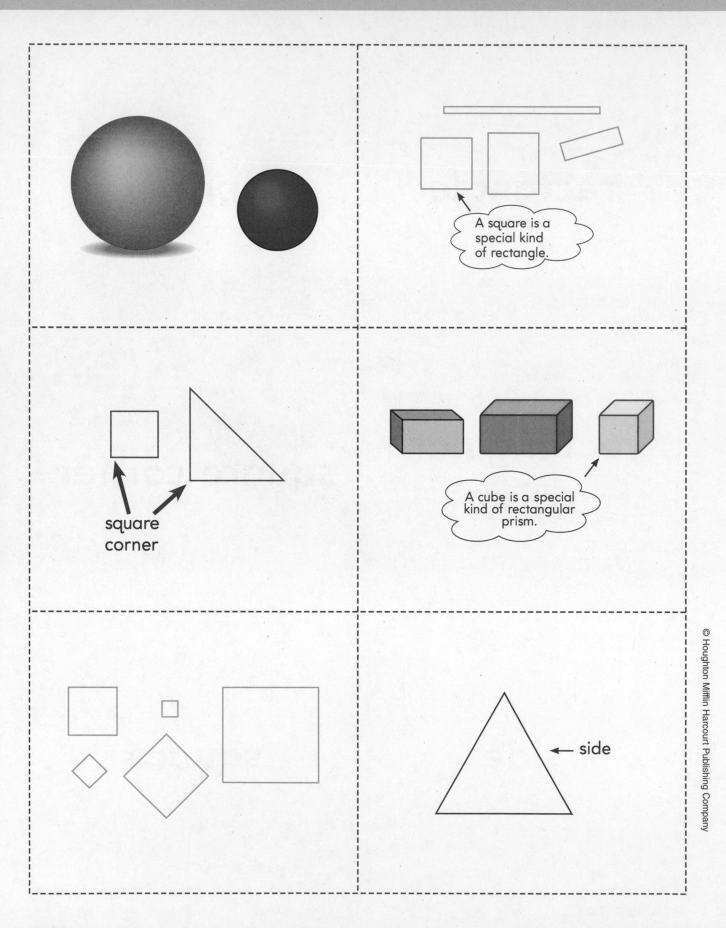

A square is a special kind of rectangle.

square corner

A cube is a special kind of rectangular prism.

side

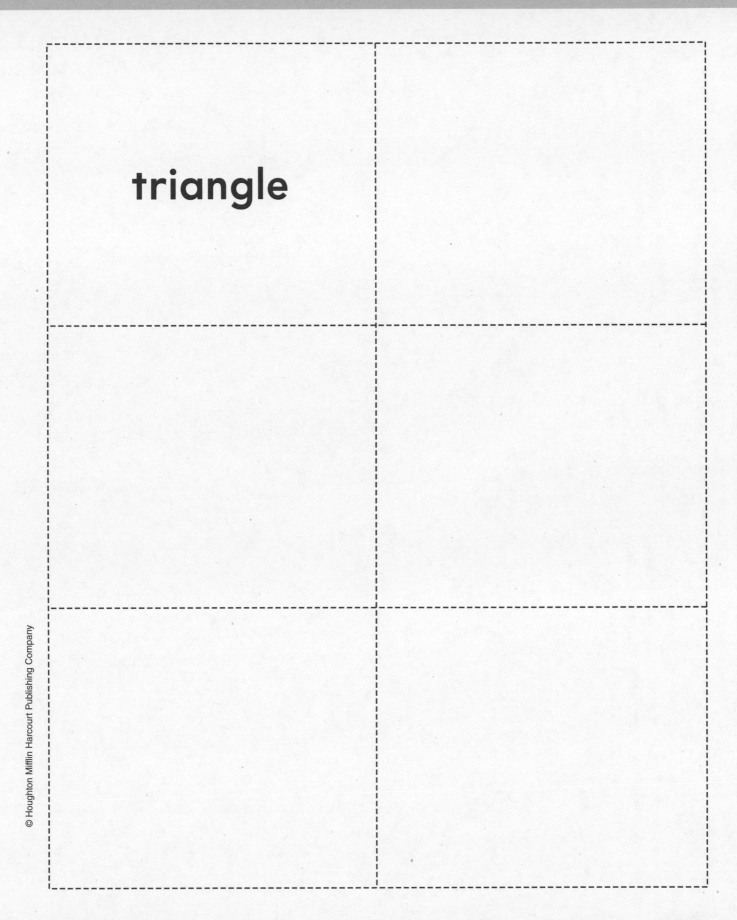

triangle

Name _____

Write the number to show the time.

1 _____ o'clock

2 _____ o'clock

3 _____ o'clock

4 _____ o'clock

5 _____ o'clock

6 _____ o'clock

Draw lines to match the time.

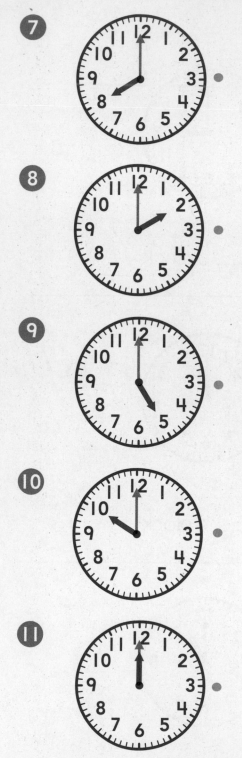

7

8

9

10

11

• 12:00

• 2:00

• 10:00

• 8:00

• 5:00

✔ **Check Understanding**

Write the digital time for 9 o'clock.

Introduction to Time

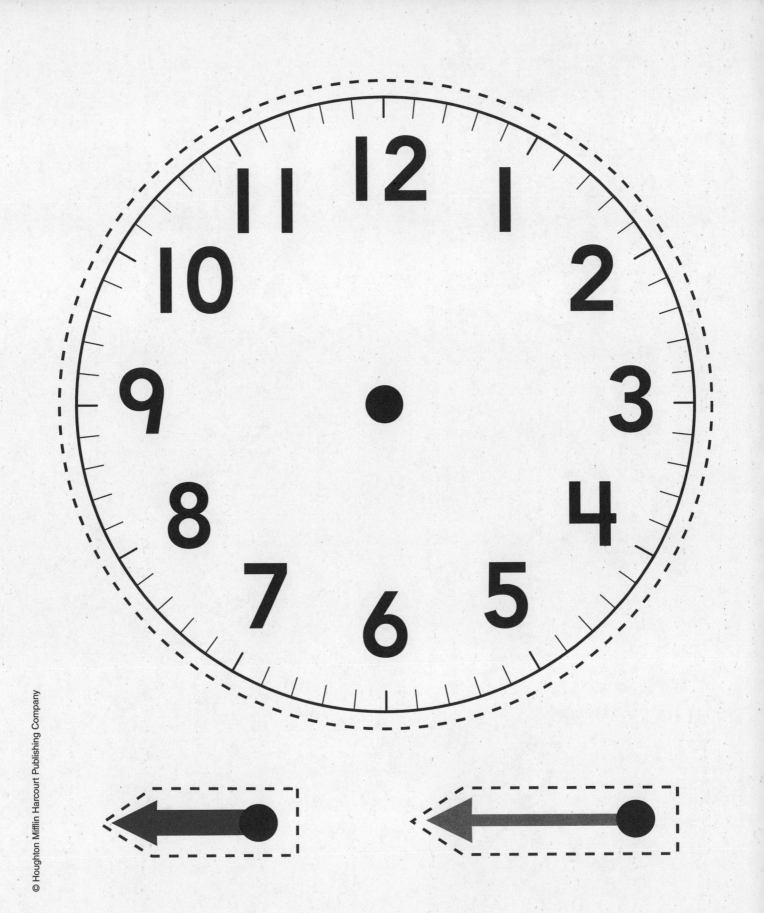

Student Clock (with hands)

Name _____

Read the **clock**.
Write the time on the digital clock.

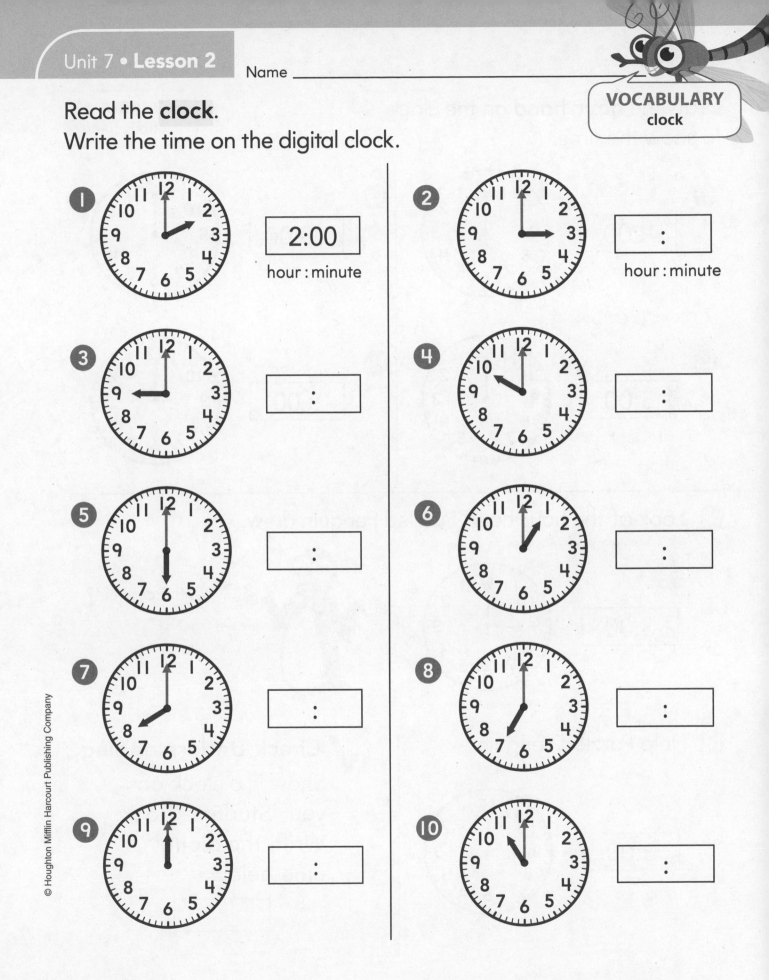

1. ☐ 2:00
   hour : minute

2. ☐ :
   hour : minute

3. ☐ :

4. ☐ :

5. ☐ :

6. ☐ :

7. ☐ :

8. ☐ :

9. ☐ :

10. ☐ :

Draw the **hour hand** on the clock
to show the time.

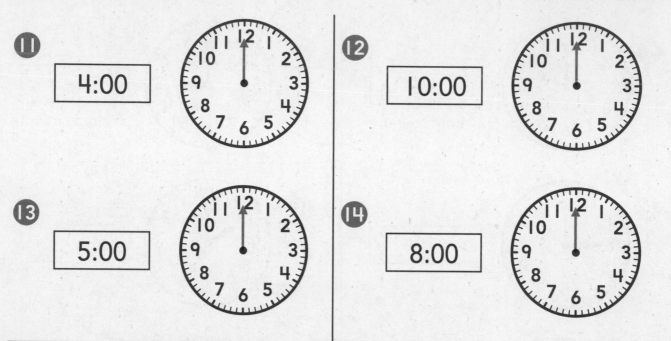

11 4:00

12 10:00

13 5:00

14 8:00

15 Look at the hour hand Puzzled Penguin drew.

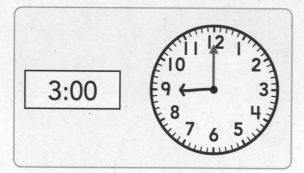

3:00

Am I correct?

16 Help Puzzled Penguin.

3:00

✔ **Check Understanding**

Show 7 o'clock on
your Student Clock.
Write the digital
time below.

Tell and Write Time in Hours

Clocks for "Our Busy Day" Book

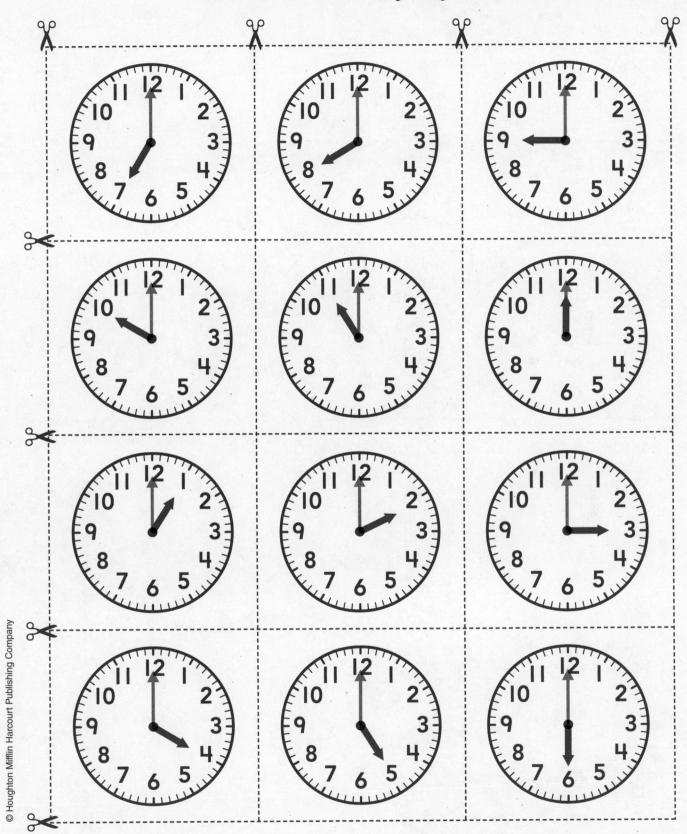

Clocks for "Our Busy Day" Book

Name _____

Read the clock.
Write the time on the digital clock.

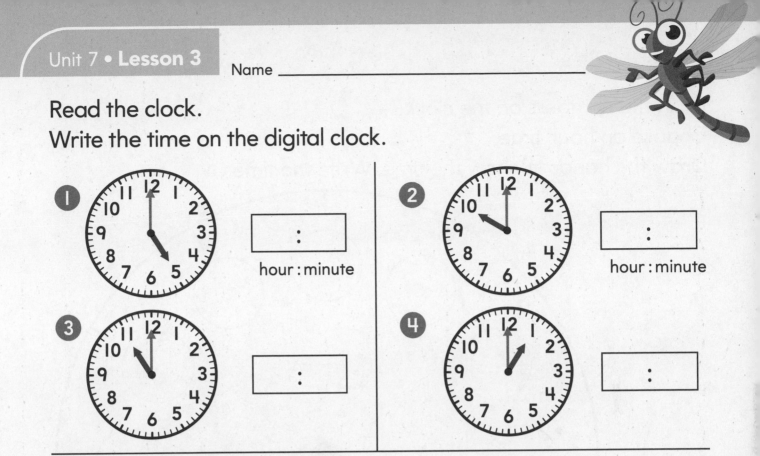

1. :
    hour : minute

2. :
    hour : minute

3. :

4. :

Draw the hour hand on the
clock to show the time.

5. 6:00

6. 9:00

7. 8:00

8. 7:00

9. 4:00

10. 3:00

Fill in the numbers on the clock.
Choose an hour time.
Draw the hands to show the time. Write the time.

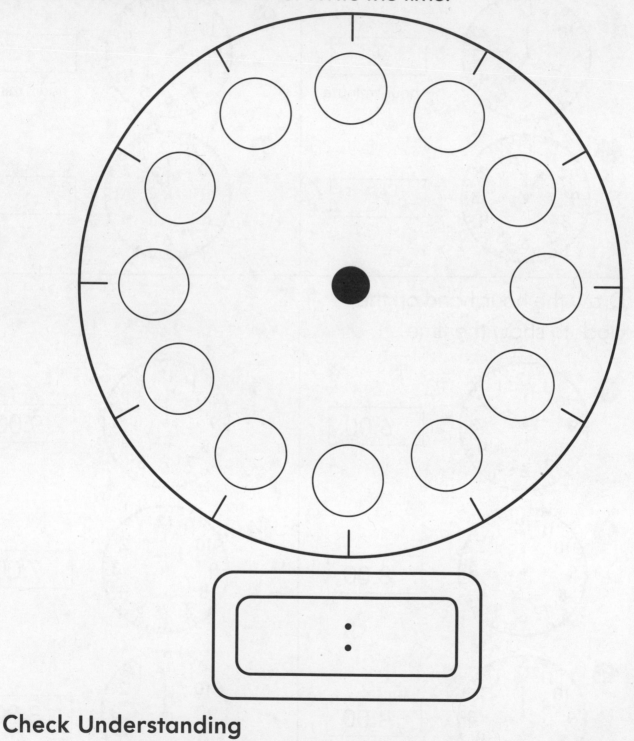

✔ **Check Understanding**

Choose another hour time and show the
time on both an analog and digital clock.

　　　　　　　　　　　　　　　Time in Our Day

Name _____

Read the clock.
Write the **half-hour** time on the digital clock.

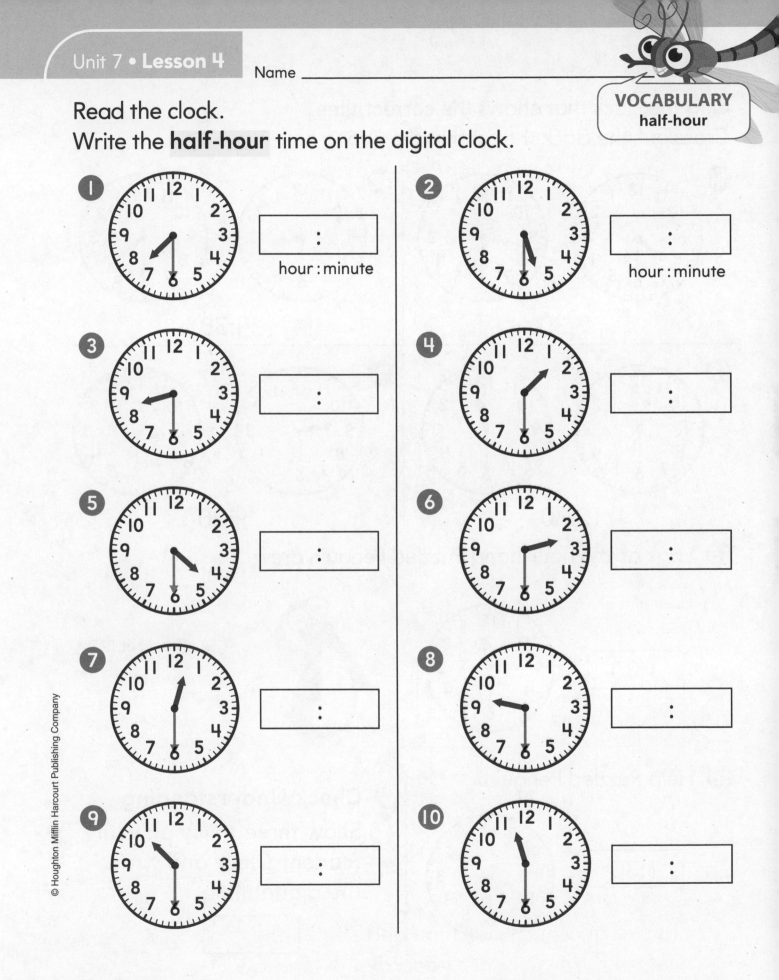

1. ☐ : ☐   hour : minute

2. ☐ : ☐   hour : minute

3. ☐ : ☐

4. ☐ : ☐

5. ☐ : ☐

6. ☐ : ☐

7. ☐ : ☐

8. ☐ : ☐

9. ☐ : ☐

10. ☐ : ☐

Ring the clock that shows the correct time.
Cross out the clock that shows the wrong time.

11   7:30

12   4:30

13   12:30

14   9:30

15 Look at the hour hand Puzzled Penguin drew.

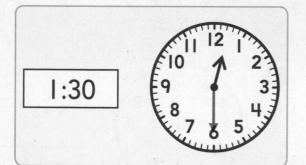

1:30

Am I correct?

16 Help Puzzled Penguin.

1:30

✓ **Check Understanding**
Show three thirty on your
Student Clock and write
the digital time.

Tell and Write Time in Half-Hours

Name _____

Show the same half-hour time on both clocks.

Practice Telling and Writing Time **321**

Show the same time on both clocks.
Pick hour and half-hour times.

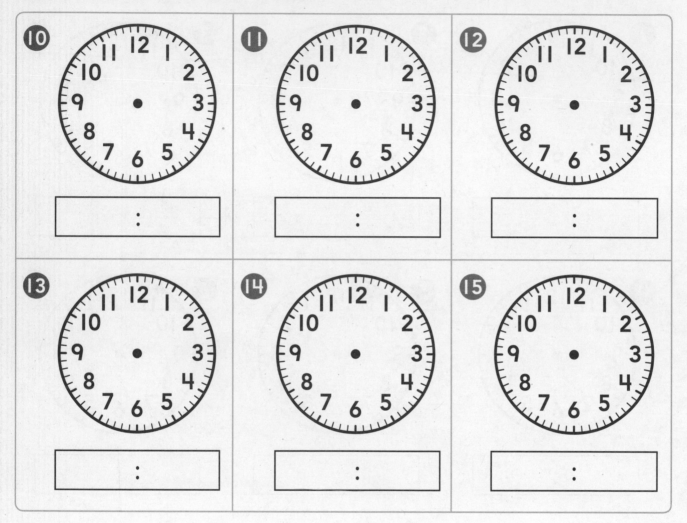

© Houghton Mifflin Harcourt Publishing Company

(PATH to FLUENCY) Find the unknown partner.

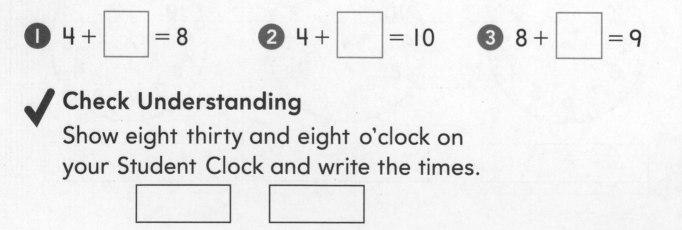

1 $4 + \boxed{} = 8$ **2** $4 + \boxed{} = 10$ **3** $8 + \boxed{} = 9$

✔ **Check Understanding**

Show eight thirty and eight o'clock on
your Student Clock and write the times.

Practice Telling and Writing Time

Read the clock.

Write the time on the digital clock.

Name _____ Date _____

PATH to FLUENCY

Add.

1 1 + 1 = ☐   **2** 5 + 3 = ☐   **3** 3 + 1 = ☐

4 5 + 5 = ☐   **5** 4 + 4 = ☐   **6** 5 + 1 = ☐

7 4 + 3 = ☐   **8** 4 + 5 = ☐   **9** 5 + 2 = ☐

Find the unknown partner.

10 1 + ☐ = 8   **11** 3 + ☐ = 6   **12** 5 + ☐ = 8

13 ☐ + 3 = 9   **14** ☐ + 5 = 10   **15** ☐ + 2 = 10

2-Dimensional Shape Set

2-Dimensional Shape Set

1 Which shapes are NOT **rectangles** or **squares**?
Draw an X on each one.

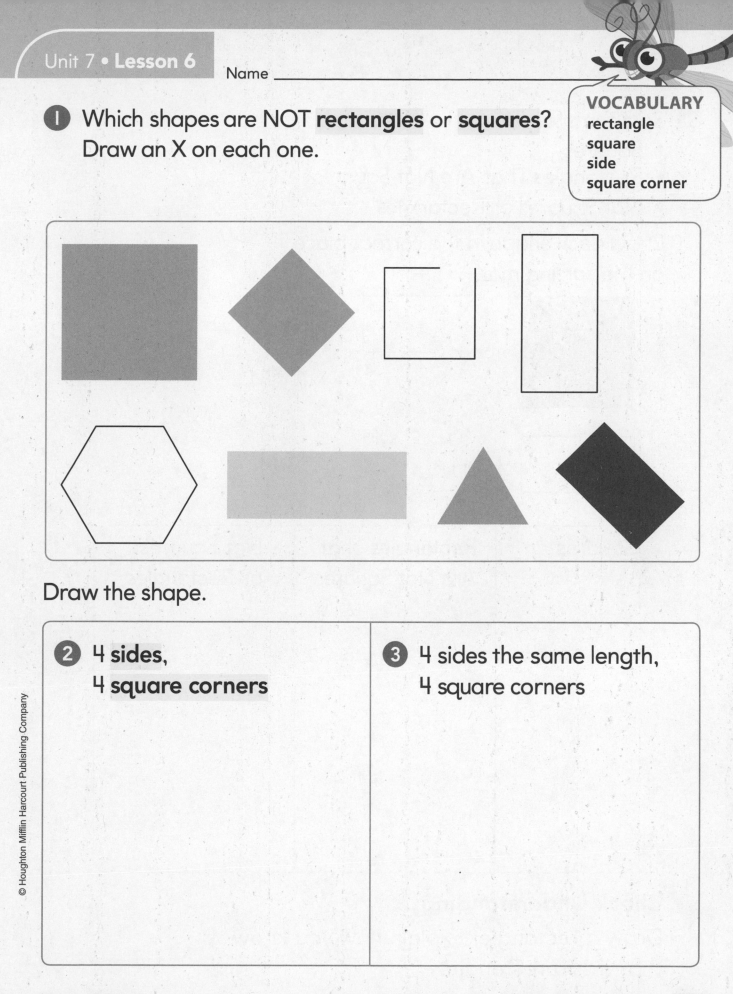

Draw the shape.

2 4 **sides**,
4 **square corners**

3 4 sides the same length,
4 square corners

4 Sort the shapes into three groups:
- Squares
- Rectangles That Are Not Squares
- Not Squares or Rectangles

Draw each shape in the correct place on the sorting mat.

Squares	Rectangles That Are Not Squares	Not Squares or Rectangles

© Houghton Mifflin Harcourt Publishing Company

✓ **Check Understanding**

Draw a rectangle. Explain how you know that it is a rectangle.

Squares and Other Rectangles

Name _____

VOCABULARY
triangle
circle

1 Which shapes are NOT **triangles** or **circles**?
Draw an X on each one.

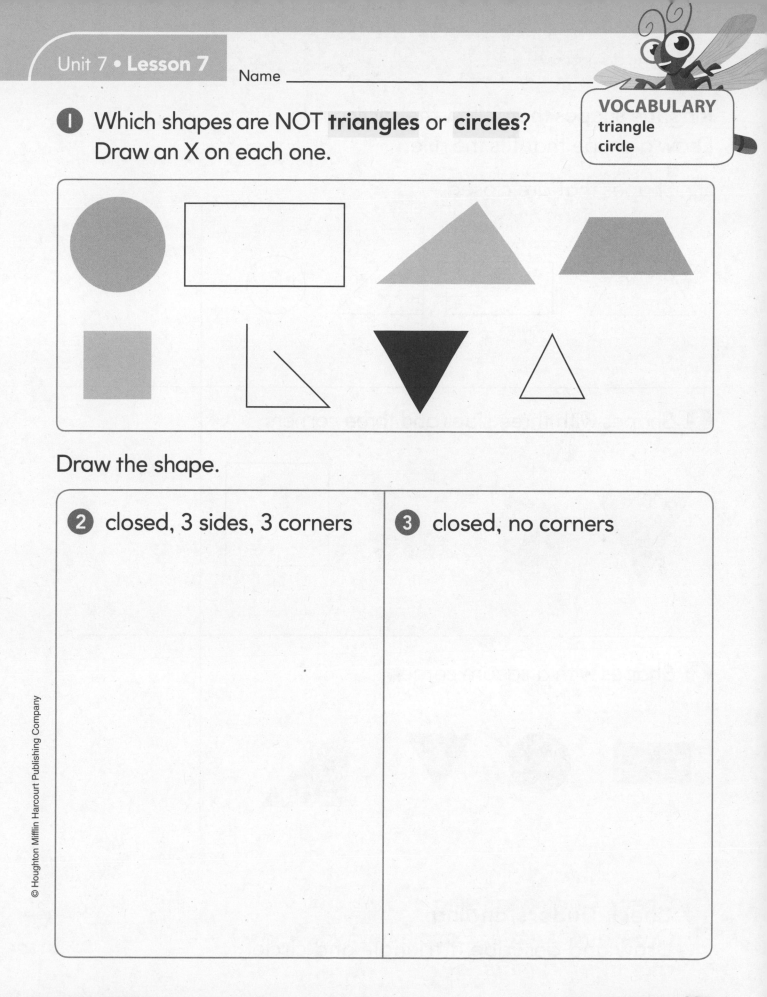

Draw the shape.

2 closed, 3 sides, 3 corners

3 closed, no corners

Triangles and Circles **331**

Ring the shapes that follow the sorting rule.
Draw a shape that fits the rule.

4 Shapes that are closed

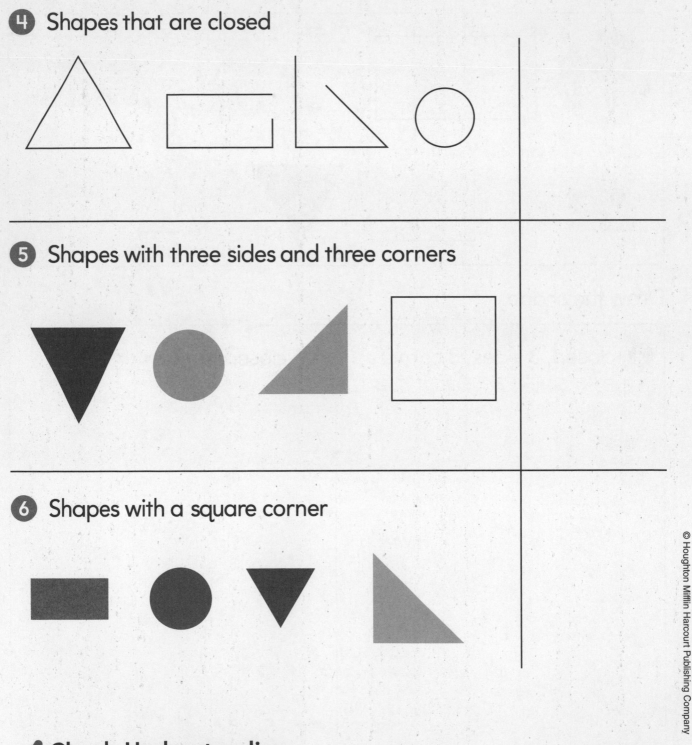

5 Shapes with three sides and three corners

6 Shapes with a square corner

✓ **Check Understanding**
Draw and describe a triangle and circle.

Triangles and Circles

Name _____

VOCABULARY
halves

Cut out the shapes below.
How many ways can you fold them into **halves**?

Equal Shares **333**

Equal Shares

Name _____

Draw a line to show halves.
Color one **half of** the shape.

VOCABULARY
half of
fourths
fourth of

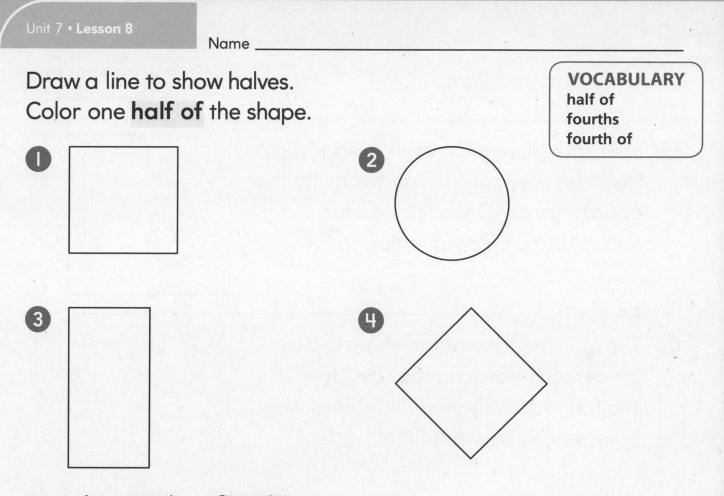

1

2

3

4

Draw lines to show **fourths**.
Color one **fourth of** the shape.

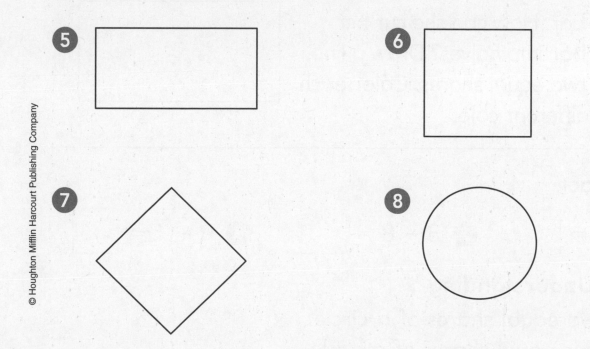

5

6

7

8

© Houghton Mifflin Harcourt Publishing Company

Equal Shares **335**

Solve the story problem.

VOCABULARY
equal shares

9 Four friends want to share a sandwich. How can they cut the sandwich into four **equal shares**? Draw lines. Color each share a different color.

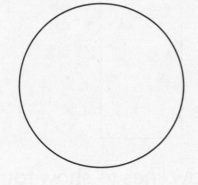

10 The four friends want to share a pie for dessert. How can they cut the pie into four equal shares? Draw lines. Color each share a different color.

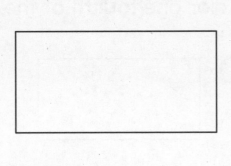

11 One friend only wants one half of her granola bar. How can she cut her granola bar into halves? Draw a line to show two equal shares. Color each share a different color.

PATH to FLUENCY Subtract.

1 $10 - 3 = \boxed{}$ **2** $8 - 8 = \boxed{}$ **3** $9 - 1 = \boxed{}$

✓ **Check Understanding**
Show two equal shares of a circle.
Show four equal shares of a circle.

© Houghton Mifflin Harcourt Publishing Company

Equal Shares

Build and draw the shape.

 Build a square. Use rectangles.

---

2 Build a rectangle with all sides the same length.
Use triangles with a square corner.

 Build a rectangle with two short sides and two
long sides. Use triangles and rectangles.

Compose 2-Dimensional Shapes

Name _____

Triangle Grid **339**

Use ▮ to make the new shape.

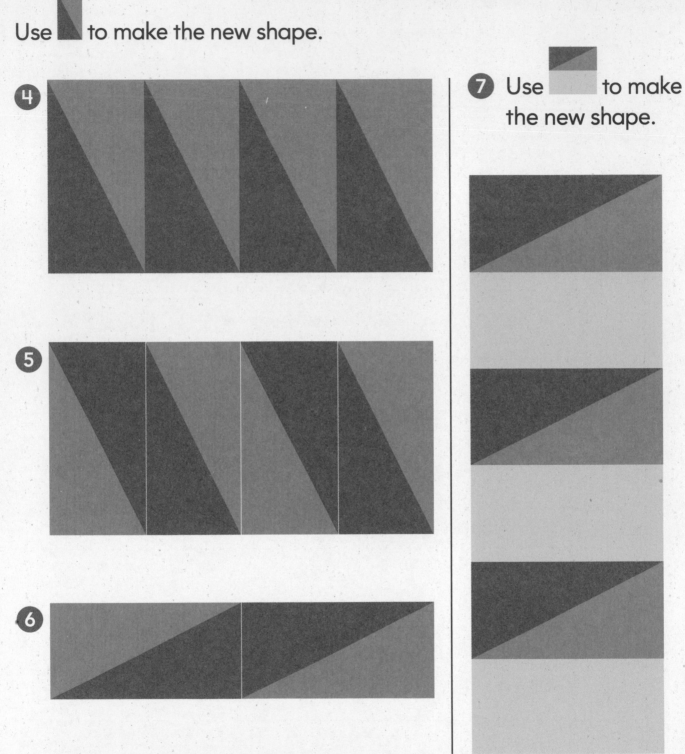

7 Use ▮ to make the new shape.

✔ **Check Understanding**
Explain how to use shapes to make a new rectangle and triangle.

Compose 2-Dimensional Shapes

Draw a line to match like shapes.
Write the name of the shape.

1 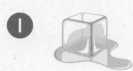 •   • ⬤ _____

2  •   • 🥫 _____

3 🏀 •   • 🎲 _____

4 👟📦 •   • 🔺 _____

5  •   • 📕 _____

6 Which shapes are NOT **rectangular prisms?**
Draw an X on each one.

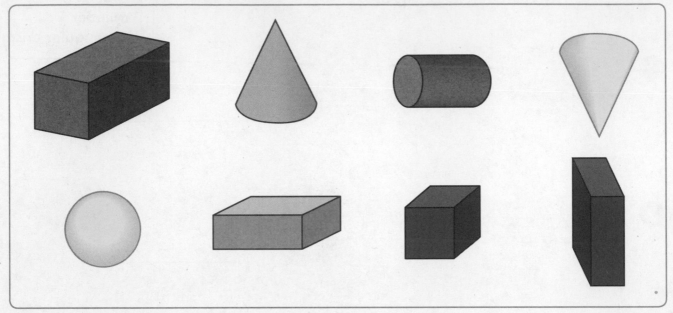

7 Ring the shapes that are **cubes**.

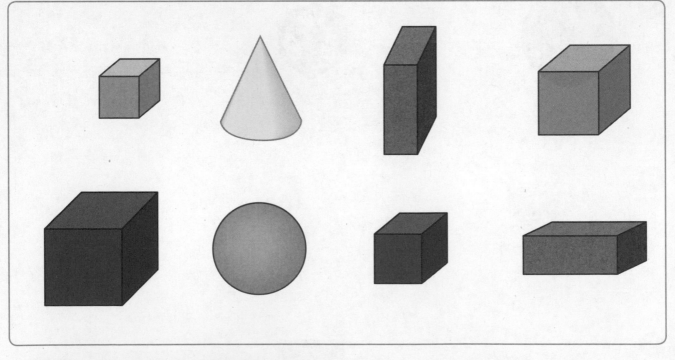

✓ **Check Understanding**
Compare a **cylinder**, a **cone**, and a
sphere. Explain what is the same and
different about the shapes.

3-Dimensional Shapes

Name _____

Ring the shapes used to make the new shape.

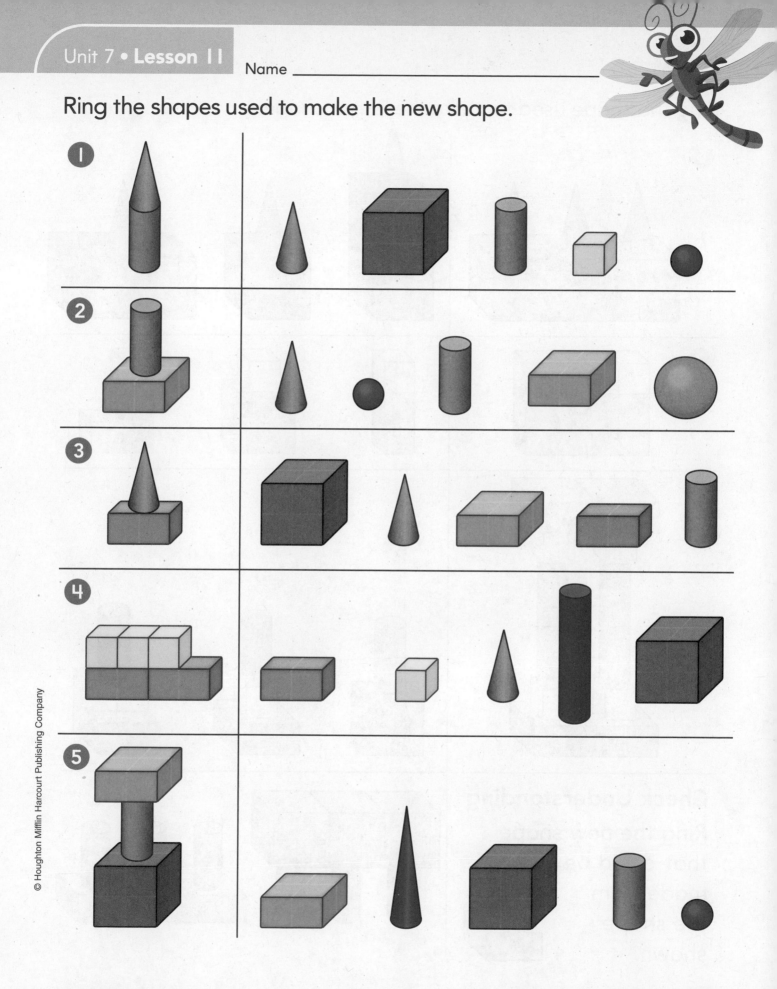

Compose 3-Dimensional Shapes **343**

Ring the shape used to make the larger shape.

6

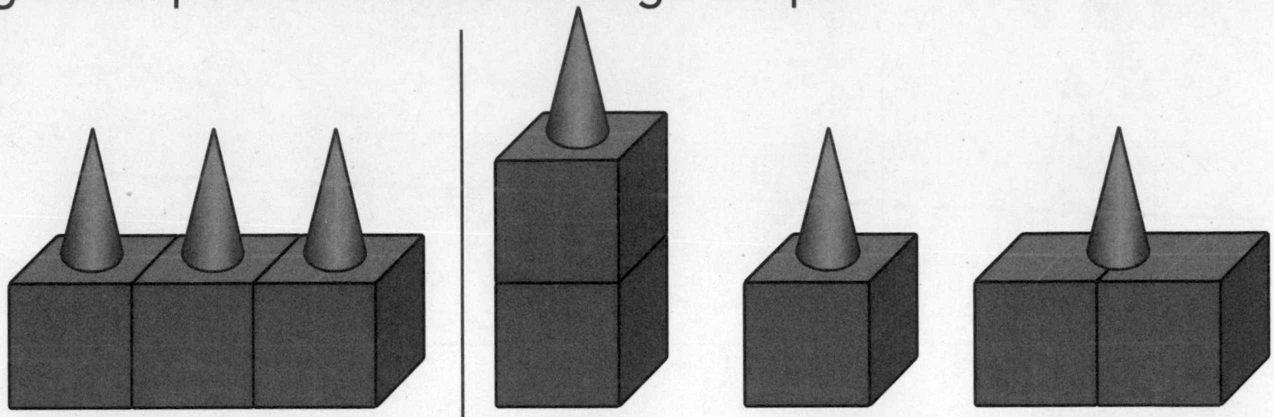

7

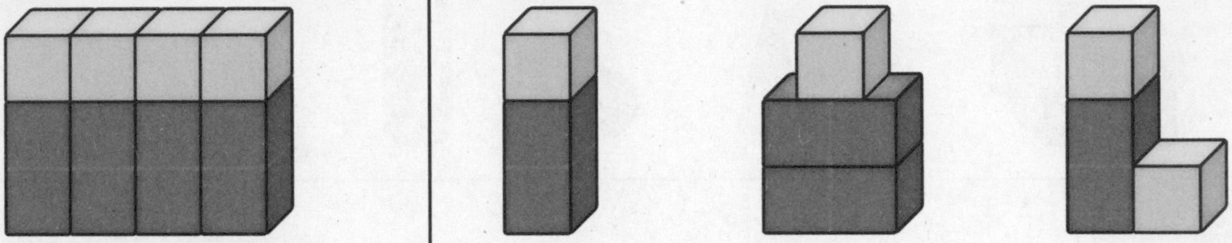

8

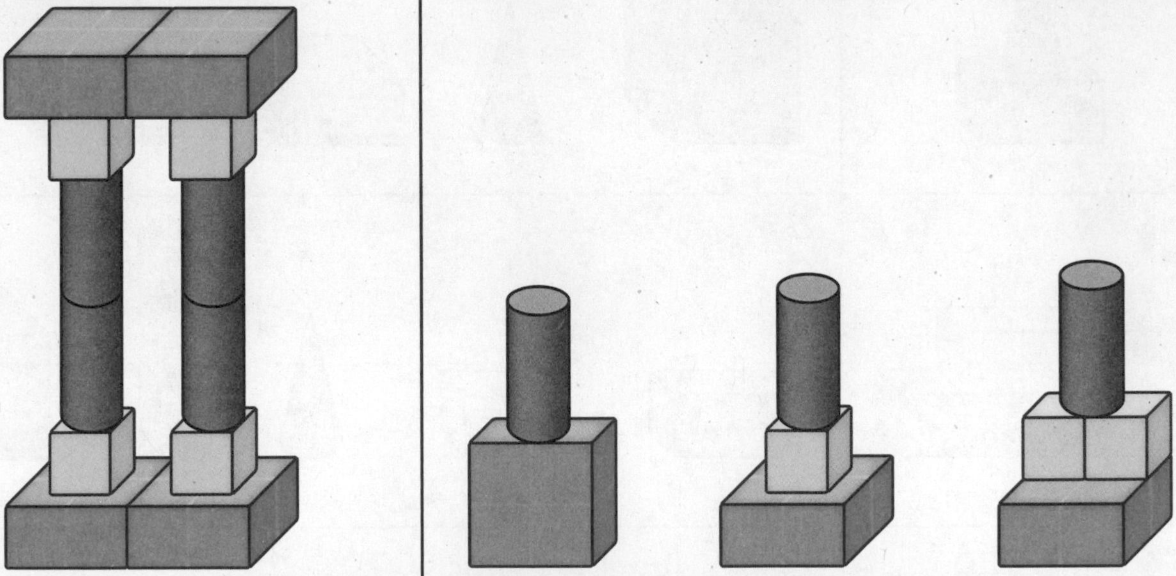

✓ **Check Understanding**

Ring the new shape that could be made from the shape shown.

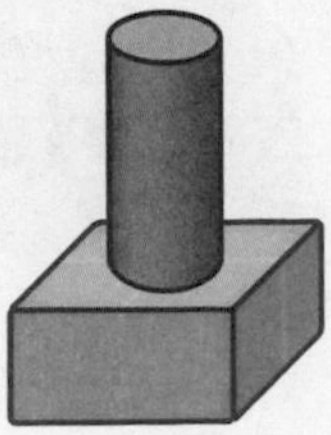

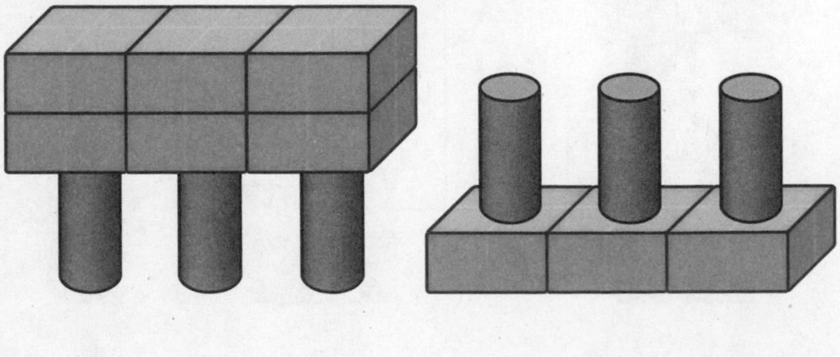

Compose 3-Dimensional Shapes

1 Draw an X on the shape that is NOT a square.

2 Ring the shapes used to make the new shape.

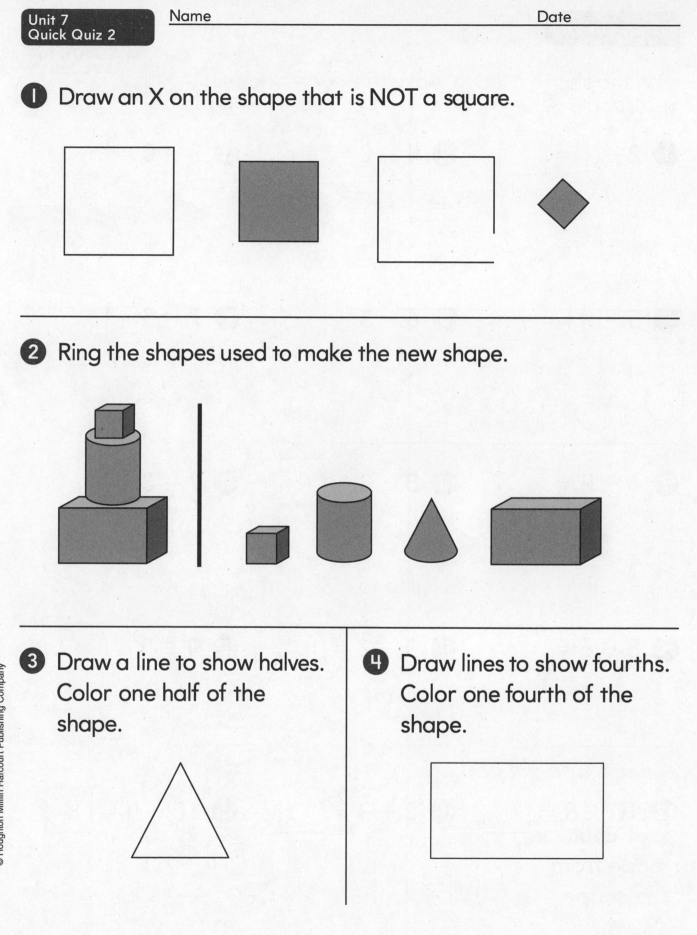

3 Draw a line to show halves. Color one half of the shape.

4 Draw lines to show fourths. Color one fourth of the shape.

Name _____ Date _____

PATH to
FLUENCY

Subtract.

1 $2 - 1 = \boxed{}$ **2** $4 - 2 = \boxed{}$ **3** $3 - 0 = \boxed{}$

4 $5 - 4 = \boxed{}$ **5** $6 - 3 = \boxed{}$ **6** $7 - 5 = \boxed{}$

7 $6 - 4 = \boxed{}$ **8** $8 - 8 = \boxed{}$ **9** $7 - 3 = \boxed{}$

10 $8 - 6 = \boxed{}$ **11** $9 - 2 = \boxed{}$ **12** $9 - 5 = \boxed{}$

13 $10 - 8 = \boxed{}$ **14** $8 - 3 = \boxed{}$ **15** $10 - 4 = \boxed{}$

Name _____

Write 1, 2, 3 to order from **shortest** to **longest**.

VOCABULARY
shortest
longest

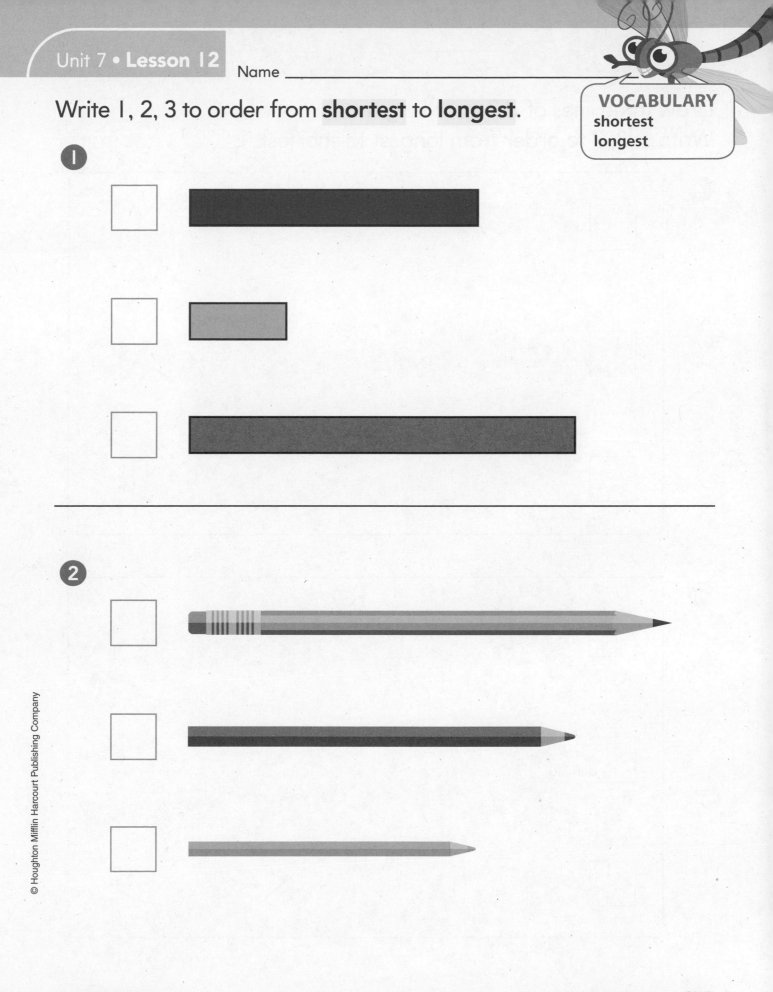

1

2

Order by Length **347**

Draw three lines of different lengths.
Write 1, 2, 3 to order from longest to shortest.

Order by Length

Name _____

Use a strip of paper to measure the blue box.
Then measure the objects with the paper strip.

5 Ring the objects that will fit in the length of the box.

Order by Length **349**

Draw to show the possible length of each object.

6 The blue box is the same length as the string.
The string is longer than the pencil.
The string is shorter than the drinking straw
and the spoon.

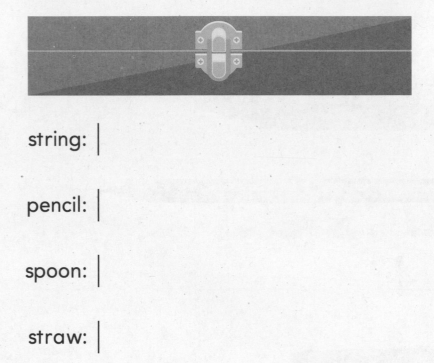

string: |

pencil: |

spoon: |

straw: |

Write the correct object.

7 The _____ will fit inside the box because
it is shorter than the box.

8 The _____ and _____ will not fit
inside the box. They are longer than the box.

✔ **Check Understanding**

Explain how to put 3 lengths of ribbon in
order from shortest to longest.

Order by Length

Name _____

Use paper clips. Measure the object.

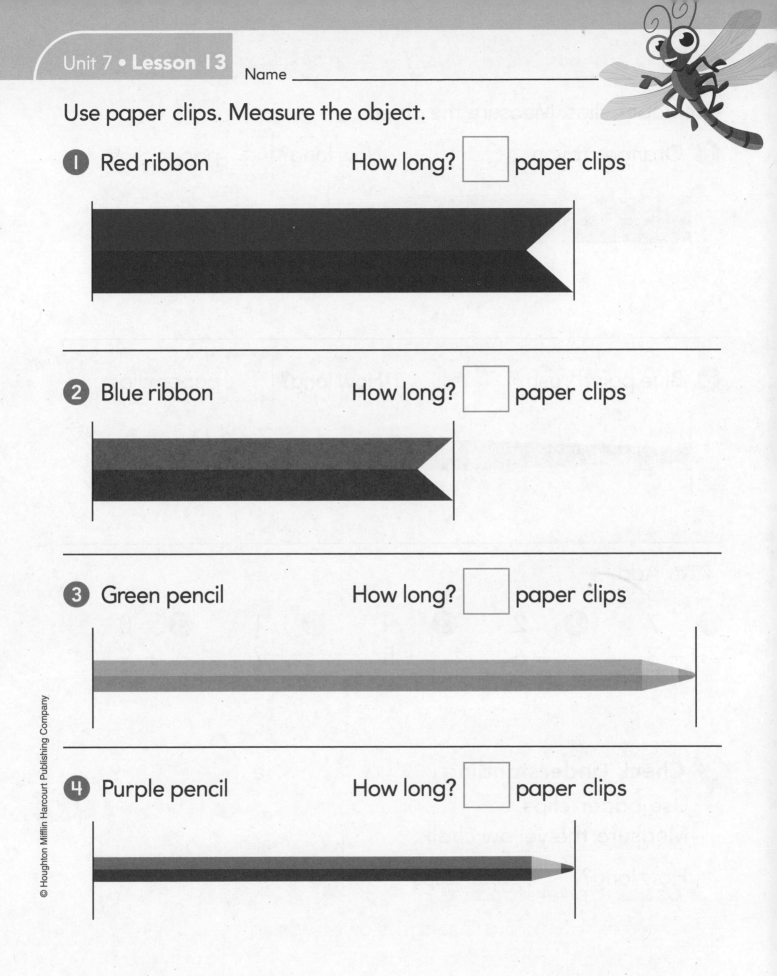

1 Red ribbon   How long? ☐ paper clips

2 Blue ribbon   How long? ☐ paper clips

3 Green pencil   How long? ☐ paper clips

4 Purple pencil   How long? ☐ paper clips

Use paper clips. Measure the object.

5 Orange crayon   How long? ☐ paper clips

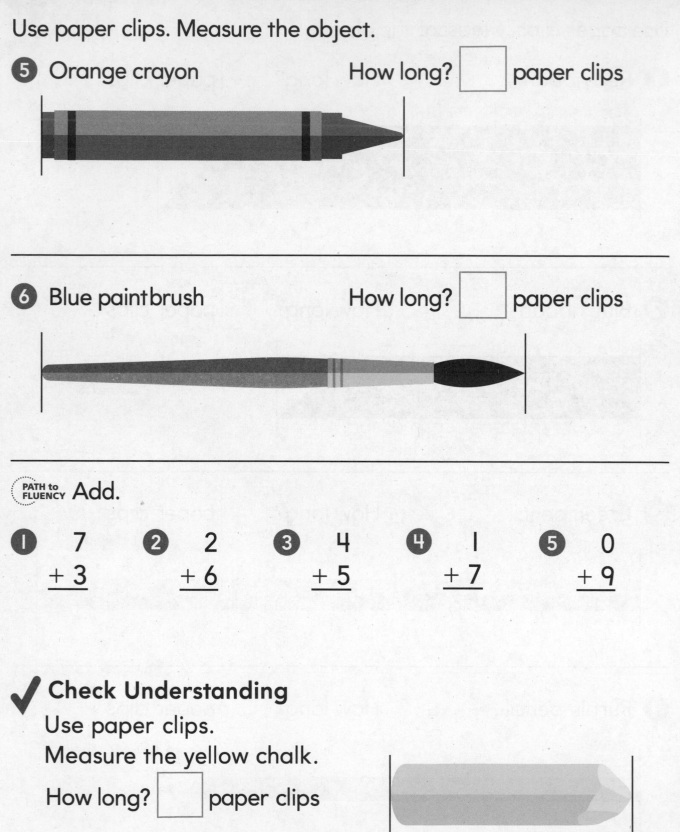

6 Blue paintbrush   How long? ☐ paper clips

PATH to FLUENCY **Add.**

1 7
    +3

2 2
    +6

3 4
    +5

4 1
    +7

5 0
    +9

✓ **Check Understanding**
Use paper clips.
Measure the yellow chalk.

How long? ☐ paper clips

Name _____

Jay and his family are going on a picnic.
Draw lines to show equal shares.

1 Jay wants to share his burger
with his mom. How can he cut
his burger into two equal shares?

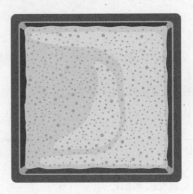

---

2 Jay and his three sisters want
to share a pan of corn bread.
How can he cut the bread into
four equal shares?

---

3 Jay's mom and his three
sisters want to share a block of
cheese. How can they cut the
block of cheese into four
equal shares?

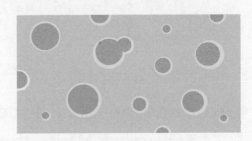

There will be lots of food at the picnic.
Measure the food in small paper clips.

4 Orange slice   How long? ☐ paper clips

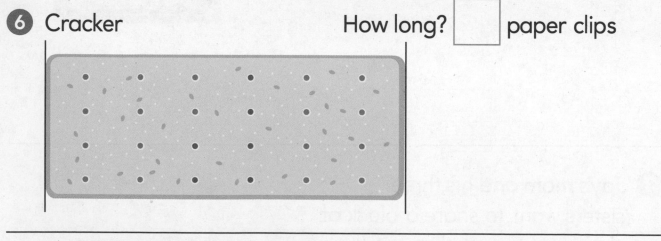

5 Celery   How long? ☐ paper clips

6 Cracker   How long? ☐ paper clips

7 Order the picnic food from longest
to shortest. Write the names.

_____

Focus on Problem Solving

Write 1, 2, 3 to order from longest to shortest.

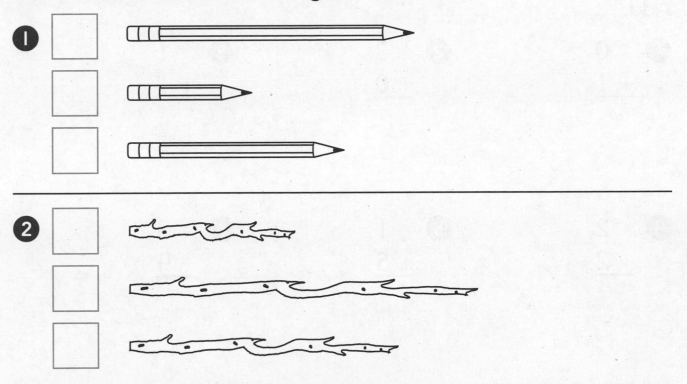

Measure in paper clips. How long?

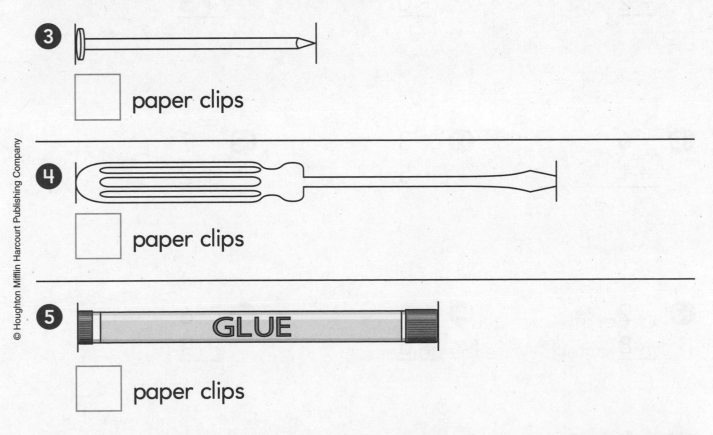

③ ☐ paper clips

④ ☐ paper clips

⑤ **GLUE**

☐ paper clips

Name _____ Date _____

Add.

1
```
   0
 + 1
```

2
```
   3
 + 0
```

3
```
   1
 + 1
```

4
```
   2
 + 2
```

5
```
   1
 + 5
```

6
```
   3
 + 4
```

7
```
   4
 + 2
```

8
```
   8
 + 0
```

9
```
   2
 + 5
```

10
```
   6
 + 1
```

11
```
   3
 + 5
```

12
```
   7
 + 2
```

13
```
   2
 + 8
```

14
```
   3
 + 6
```

15
```
   6
 + 4
```

Read the clock.

Write the time on the digital clock.

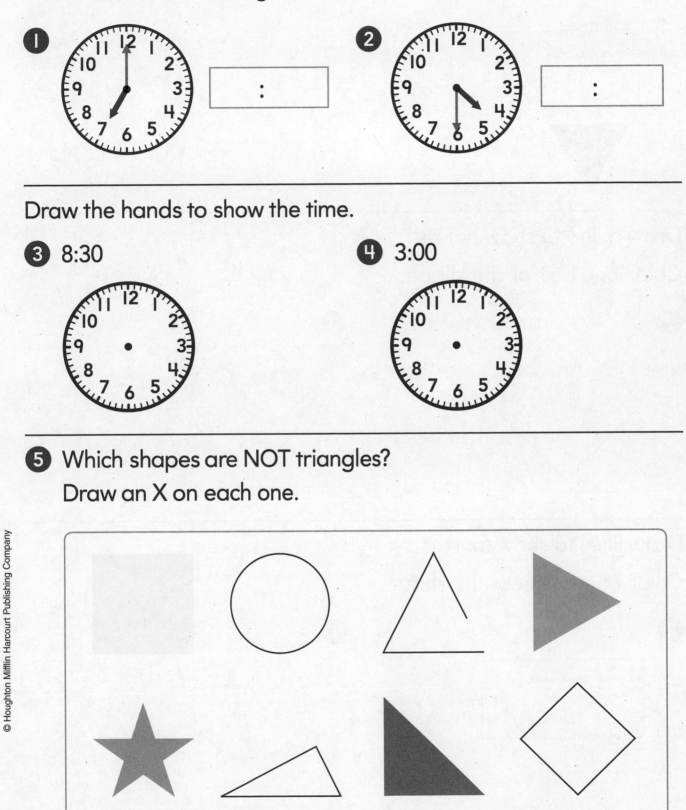

1

☐ : ☐

2

☐ : ☐

Draw the hands to show the time.

3 8:30

4 3:00

5 Which shapes are NOT triangles?
Draw an X on each one.

6 Is the shape a square? Choose Yes or No.

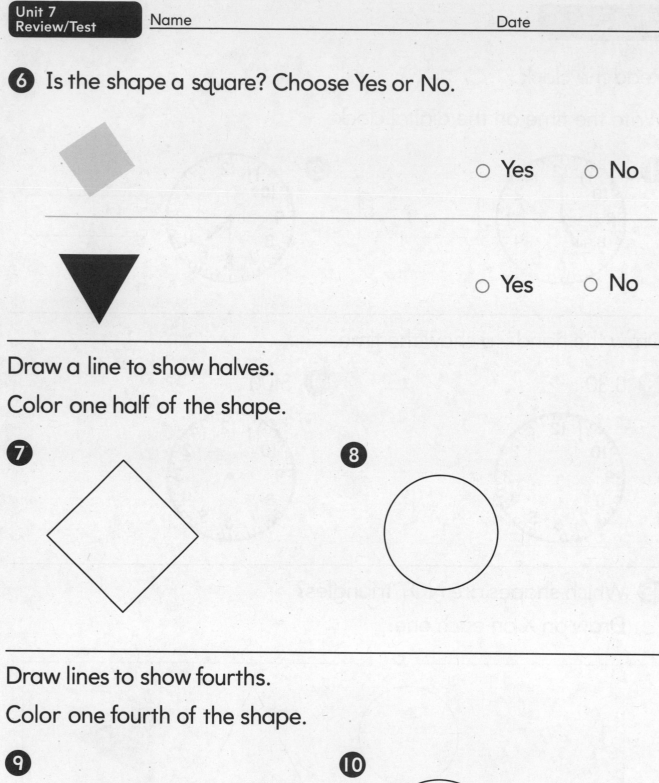

○ Yes   ○ No

○ Yes   ○ No

Draw a line to show halves.

Color one half of the shape.

7

8

Draw lines to show fourths.

Color one fourth of the shape.

9

10

11 Draw a line from the shape to its name.

•   • rectangular prism

•   • sphere

•   • cylinder

12 Choose the shapes used to make the new shape.

○   ○   ○   ○

13 Choose the shape used to make the larger shape.

○   ○   ○

14 Measure in paper clips.

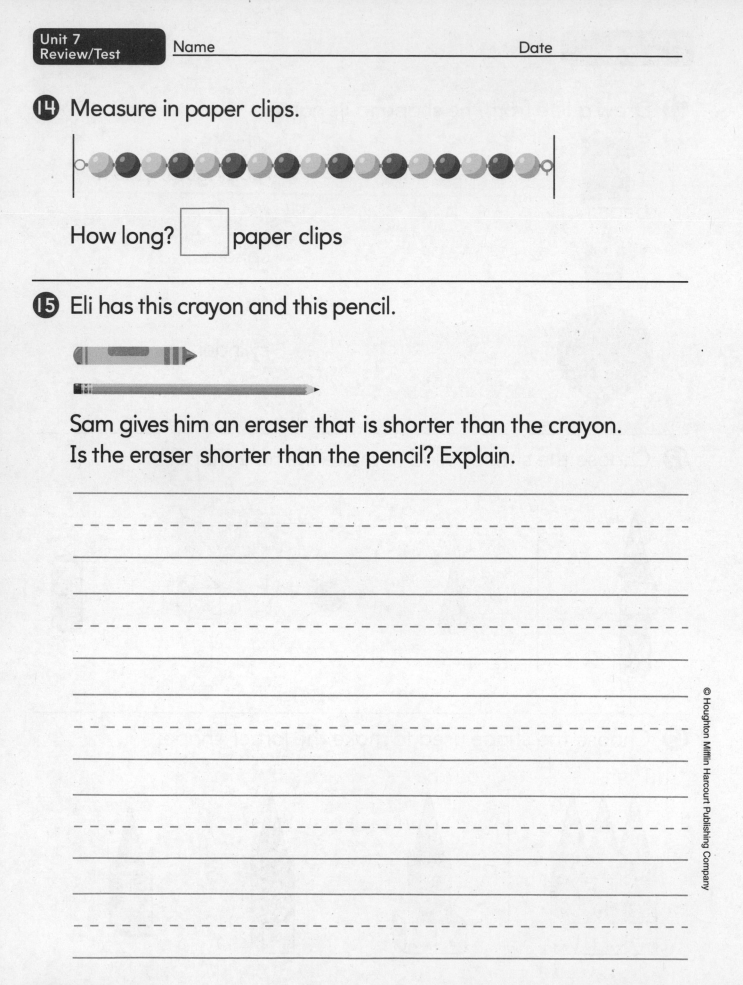

How long? ☐ paper clips

---

15 Eli has this crayon and this pencil.

Sam gives him an eraser that is shorter than the crayon.
Is the eraser shorter than the pencil? Explain.

Busy Bug's Day

1 **Part A**

The clock hands show Busy Bug's bedtime.

Write the same time on the digital clock.

Part B Tell how you know what time it is.

2 **Part A** This is the shape of Busy Bug's snack.

He wants to share his snack with three friends.

Draw lines to show fourths.

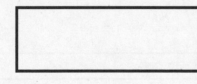

Part B Tell how you know the parts are fourths.

Busy Bug's Day (continued)

3 **Part A** Busy Bug likes only squares. Help him find the squares. Draw an X on each shape that is NOT a square.

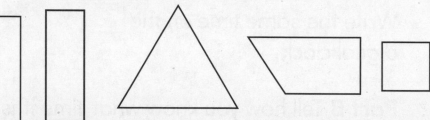

Part B Tell how you know a shape is a square.

4 **Part A**

This is Busy Bug's walking stick.

This is Busy Bug's bed.

How many paper clips long is the bed?

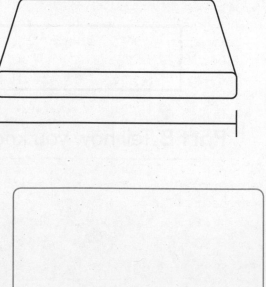

☐ _____

Part B

Busy Bug's table is longer than his walking stick. It is shorter than his bed. Draw Busy Bug's table.

Dear Family:

Your child will be using special drawings of 10-sticks and circles to add greater numbers. The sticks show the number of tens, and the circles show the number of ones. When a new group of ten is made, a ring is drawn around it.

There are several ways for children to show the new group of ten when they add 2-digit numbers.

• Children can do the addition with a single total. The 1 for the new ten can be written either below the tens column or above it. Writing it below makes addition easier because the 1 new ten is added after children have added the two numbers that are already there. Also, children can see the 16 they made from 7 and 9 because the 1 and 6 are closer together than they were when the new ten was written above.

$$
\begin{array}{r}
27 \\
+\,4\overset{1}{9} \\
\hline
76
\end{array}
\quad \text{new ten below}
$$

$$
\begin{array}{r}
\overset{1}{2}7 \\
+\,49 \\
\hline
76
\end{array}
\quad \text{new ten above}
$$

• Children can make separate totals for tens and ones. Many first-graders prefer to work from left to right because that is how they read. They add the tens (20 + 40 = 60) and then the ones (7 + 9 = 16). The last step is to add the two totals together (60 + 16 = 76).

$$
\begin{array}{r}
27 \\
+\,49 \\
\hline
60 \\
16 \\
\hline
76
\end{array}
\qquad
\begin{array}{r}
27 \\
+\,49 \\
\hline
16 \\
60 \\
\hline
76
\end{array}
$$

left to right   right to left

You may notice your child using one of these methods as he or she completes homework.

Sincerely,
Your child's teacher

Estimada familia:

Su niño usará dibujos especiales de palitos de decenas y círculos para sumar números más grandes. Los palitos muestran el número de decenas y los círculos muestran el número de unidades. Cuando se forma un nuevo grupo de diez, se encierra.

Hay varias maneras en las que los niños pueden mostrar el nuevo grupo de diez al sumar números de 2 dígitos.

- Pueden hacer la suma con un total único. El 1 que indica la nueva decena se puede escribir abajo o arriba de la columna de las decenas. Escribirlo abajo hace que la suma sea más fácil porque la nueva decena se suma después de sumar los dos números que ya estaban allí. Además, los niños pueden ver el 16 que obtuvieron de 7 y 9 porque el 1 y el 6 están más juntos que cuando la nueva decena estaba escrita arriba.

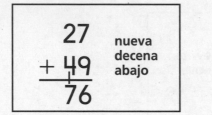

- Pueden hacer totales separados para decenas y para unidades. Muchos estudiantes de primer grado prefieren trabajar de izquierda a derecha porque así leen. Suman las decenas (20 + 40 = 60) y luego las unidades (7 + 9 = 16). El último paso es sumar ambos totales (60 + 16 = 76).

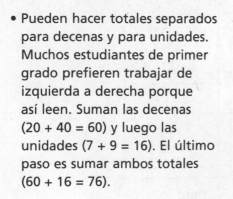

Es posible que su niño use uno de estos métodos al hacer la tarea.

Atentamente,
El maestro de su niño

Name _____

Draw circles to show the apples.

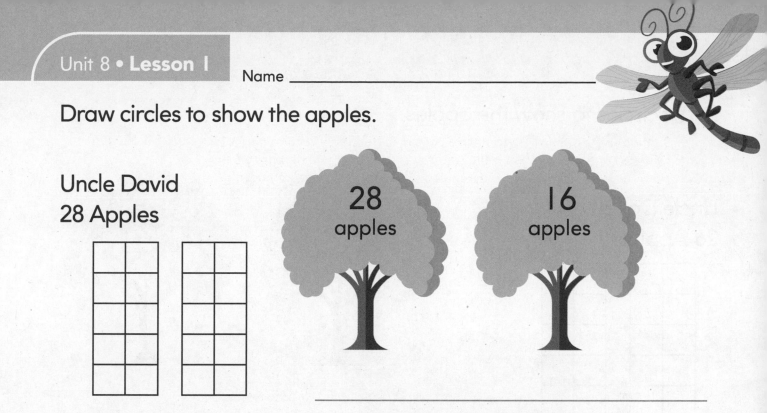

**Uncle David
28 Apples**

28 apples

16 apples

Put extra apples here.

**Aunt Sarah
16 Apples**

Put extra apples here.

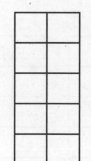

Total Apples

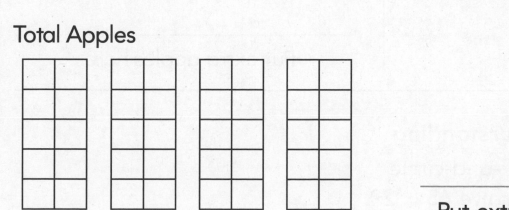

Put extra apples here.

Draw circles to show the apples.

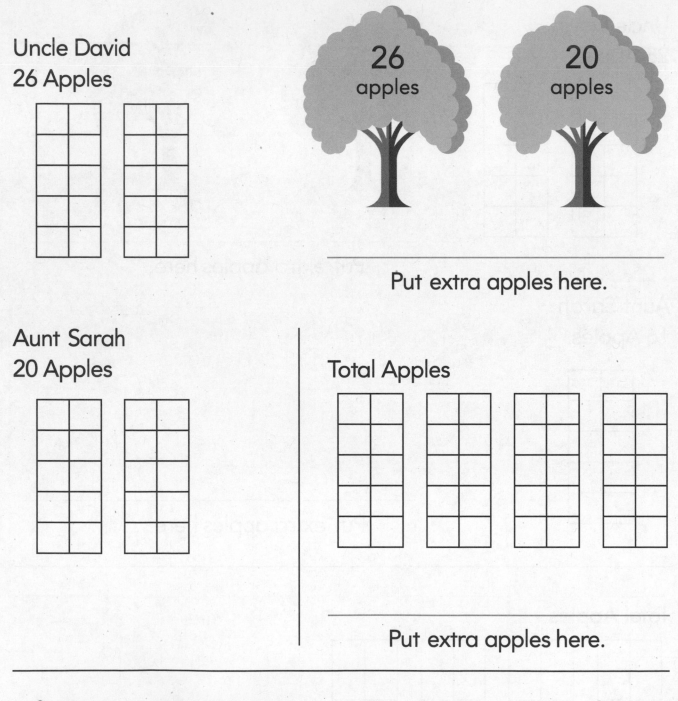

Uncle David
26 Apples

26 apples

20 apples

Put extra apples here.

Aunt Sarah
20 Apples

Total Apples

Put extra apples here.

✔ **Check Understanding**
Make a stick-and-circle
drawing to solve 65 + 29.

Explore 2-Digit Addition

Name _____

47 apples

19 apples

26 apples

13 apples

25 apples

34 apples

51 apples

29 apples

37 apples

48 apples

1. Work in pairs. Each child chooses one apple tree.

2. On your MathBoard or paper, add the number of apples in the two trees.

3. Check to see if you both got the same answer.

4. Repeat with other trees.

24 apples

36 apples

9 apples

30 apples

5 apples

20 apples

40 apples

2 apples

19 apples

53 apples

5 Work in pairs. One child chooses one apple tree with a 2-digit number. The other child chooses another tree.

6 On your MathBoard or paper, add the apples in the two trees.

7 Check to see if you both got the same answer.

✓ **Check Understanding**

Use the New Group Below method to solve 55 + 36.

Methods of 2-Digit Addition

Name _____

Write the numbers to show addition.

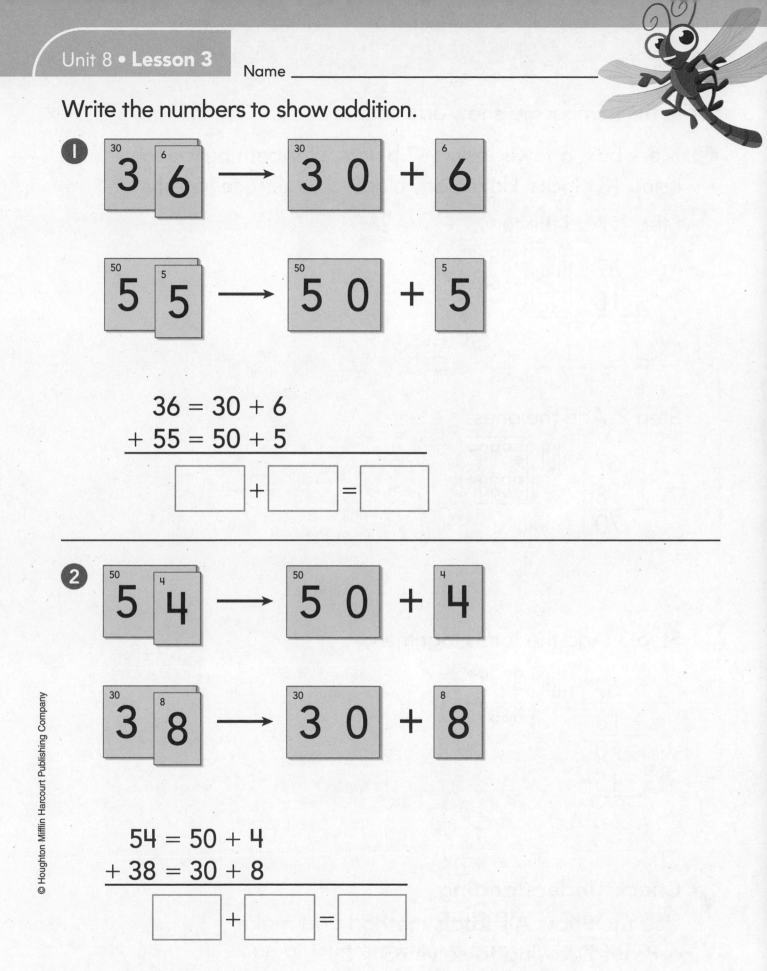

1

30 3 6 6 → 30 3 0 + 6 6

50 5 5 5 → 50 5 0 + 5 5

$$36 = 30 + 6$$
$$+\ 55 = 50 + 5$$

⬚ + ⬚ = ⬚

2

50 5 4 4 → 50 5 0 + 4 4

30 3 8 8 → 30 3 0 + 8 8

$$54 = 50 + 4$$
$$+\ 38 = 30 + 8$$

⬚ + ⬚ = ⬚

Addition of Tens and Ones **369**

Write the numbers to show addition.

3 Mark built a tower using 67 blocks. Elizabeth built a tower using 18 blocks. How many blocks did they use together?

Step 1: Add the tens.

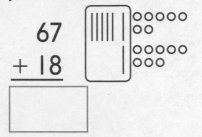

```
  67
+ 18
┌─────┐
│     │
└─────┘
```

Step 2: Add the ones.

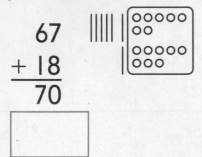

```
  67
+ 18
  70
┌─────┐
│     │
└─────┘
```

Step 3: Add the totals together.

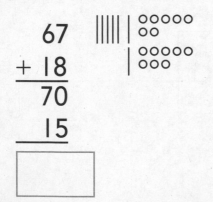

```
  67
+ 18
  70
  15
┌─────┐
│     │
└─────┘
```

 Check Understanding

Use the Show All Totals method and make a Proof Drawing to solve 63 + 28.

Addition of Tens and Ones

Name _____

28 peaches

35 peaches

42 peaches

48 peaches

47 peaches

50 peaches

16 peaches

49 peaches

27 peaches

43 peaches

1 Work in pairs. Each child chooses one peach tree.

2 On your MathBoard or paper, add the number of peaches in the two trees.

3 Check to see if you both got the same answer.

4 Repeat with other trees.

5 For which problems did you make a new ten?

Add.

6 53
   + 38

7 16
   + 6

8 67
   + 15

9 72
   + 20

10 56
    + 13

11 47
    + 30

12 48
    + 5

13 82
    + 14

14 17
    + 2

Write the vertical form. Then add.

15 65 + 8

16 56 + 28

17 6 + 73

✓ **Check Understanding**
Use two different methods to solve 15 + 18.

Discuss Solution Methods

Name _____

Add.

1
$$\begin{array}{r} 93 \\ +\ 6 \\ \hline \end{array}$$

2
$$\begin{array}{r} 28 \\ +18 \\ \hline \end{array}$$

3
$$\begin{array}{r} 66 \\ +\ 7 \\ \hline \end{array}$$

4
$$\begin{array}{r} 49 \\ +30 \\ \hline \end{array}$$

5
$$\begin{array}{r} 56 \\ +25 \\ \hline \end{array}$$

6
$$\begin{array}{r} 15 \\ +\ 4 \\ \hline \end{array}$$

Write the vertical form. Then add.

7 $71 + 19$

8 $54 + 20$

9 $33 + 29$

10 $44 + 4$

11 $8 + 74$

12 $19 + 67$

Practice 2-Digit Addition **373**

13 Look at the total Puzzled Penguin wrote.

```
  43
+ 39
-----
 712
```

Am I correct?

14 Help Puzzled Penguin.

```
  43
+ 39
-----
```

PATH to FLUENCY Add.

1 5 + 2 = ☐

2 7 + 1 = ☐

3 3 + 2 = ☐

4 ☐ = 8 + 2

5 ☐ = 3 + 6

6 ☐ = 4 + 3

7 5 + 1 = ☐

8 6 + 2 = ☐

9 5 + 3 = ☐

10 ☐ = 7 + 2

11 ☐ = 4 + 2

12 ☐ = 2 + 1

✔ **Check Understanding**

Write 26 + 18 as a vertical form and solve.

Practice 2-Digit Addition

Name _____

Use the pictures to solve. Show your work.

① How many potatoes are there?

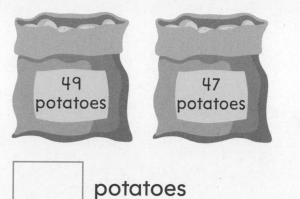

☐ potatoes

② How many cartons of milk are there?

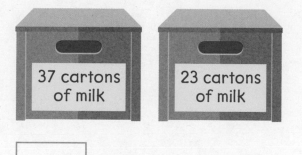

☐ cartons of milk

③ 20 cartons of milk spill.
How many cartons of milk are there now?

☐ cartons of milk

Use the pictures to solve. Show your work.

4 How many jars of honey are there?

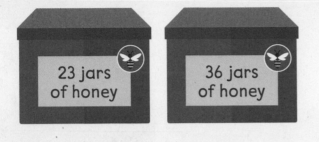

23 jars of honey   36 jars of honey

☐ jars of honey

5 How many jars of jam are there?

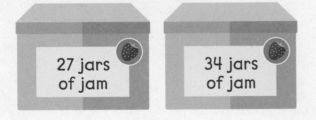

27 jars of jam   34 jars of jam

☐ jars of jam

6 Compare the number of jars of honey to the number of jars of jam. Write the comparison 2 ways.

☐ ◯ ☐

☐ ◯ ☐

Focus on Problem Solving

Name ________________________ Date ____________

Add.

1. $\begin{array}{r} 27 \\ +\ \ 5 \\ \hline \end{array}$

2. $\begin{array}{r} 43 \\ +\ 30 \\ \hline \end{array}$

3. $\begin{array}{r} 58 \\ +\ 26 \\ \hline \end{array}$

Write the vertical form. Then add.

4. 29 + 34

---

5. 38 + 6

Name _____ Date _____

Add.

1 2 + 2 = ☐   **2** 3 + 3 = ☐   **3** 1 + 3 = ☐

4 3 + 2 = ☐   **5** 4 + 3 = ☐   **6** 1 + 7 = ☐

7 2 + 4 = ☐   **8** 4 + 6 = ☐   **9** 6 + 2 = ☐

10 7 + 2 = ☐   **11** 5 + 4 = ☐   **12** 7 + 3 = ☐

13 ☐ = 3 + 5   **14** ☐ = 2 + 8   **15** ☐ = 5 + 4

Solve. Group ones to make tens.

1 Grace has 18 apples.   Jake has 24 apples.

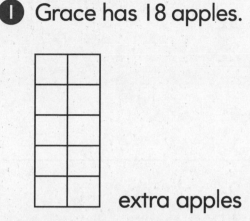

extra apples

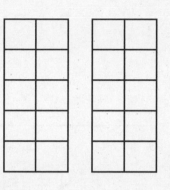

extra apples

How many apples do they have?

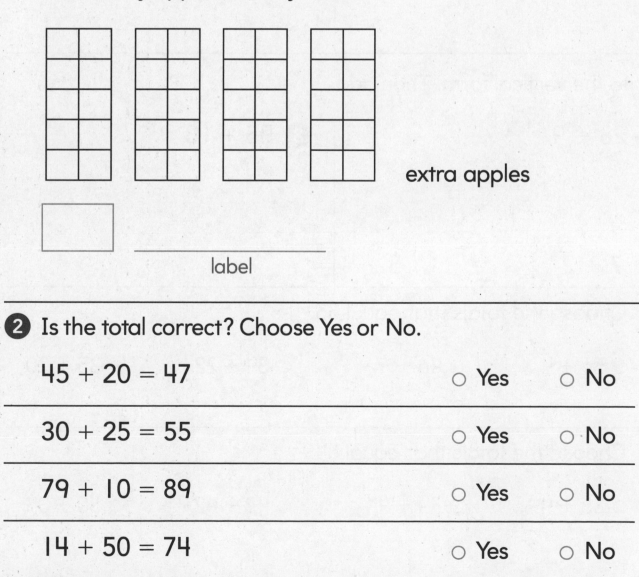

extra apples

_____
label

2 Is the total correct? Choose Yes or No.

$45 + 20 = 47$	○ Yes	○ No
$30 + 25 = 55$	○ Yes	○ No
$79 + 10 = 89$	○ Yes	○ No
$14 + 50 = 74$	○ Yes	○ No

Name _____   Date _____

Add.

3 63
    + 29
_____

4 52
    + 20
_____

5 78
    + 5
_____

6 26
    + 15
_____

Write the vertical form. Then add.

7 28 + 9

8 45 + 18

9 Choose the totals that equal 55.

  ○ 51 + 4   ○ 46 + 9   ○ 34 + 22   ○ 35 + 20

10 Choose the totals that equal 84.

  ○ 35 + 49   ○ 34 + 44   ○ 42 + 42   ○ 50 + 34

11 How many apples are there?
Show your work.

54
apples

29
apples

[ ]
_____
label

Choose the correct answer.

12 57 + 15

○ 62

○ 68

○ 72

○ 82

13 51 + 40

⊖ 55

○ 71

○ 91

○ 95

14 How many peaches are there?
Show your work.

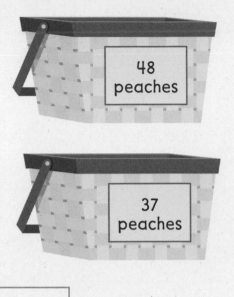

48 peaches

37 peaches

[ ] _____
        label

---

15 Write an addition exercise that you must make a new ten to solve. Use two 2-digit numbers. Make a Proof Drawing.

How Many Pears?

Some friends pick pears.

Choose one of the numbers below for each ◯.
Use each number only one time.

9   16   27   35

1 Lisa picks more pears than Rena.
Together they pick 36 pears.
How many does each girl pick?

Lisa picks ◯ pears.

Rena picks ◯ pears.

Show how you know.

2 Luis and Tran pick ◯ pears.
Then they pick 20 more pears.
What is the total number of
pears they pick?

[ ] pears

Show how you know.

3 Maya picks ◯ pears. Vinny
picks 15 pears. How many
pears do they pick in all?

[ ] pears

Show how you know.

How Many Pears? (continued)

4 Jamal picks 38 pears.
His grandma picks 24 pears.
How many pears do they pick
altogether?

Show and tell how you know.

[   ] pears

---

5 Kat picks 25 pears. Alex picks
19 pears. They want to find how
many pears they pick altogether.
Look at the total.

```
   25
 + 19
 ─────
   3̶1̶4̶
```

Tell why the total is not correct.
Find the correct total.

Addition and Subtraction Problem Types

	Result Unknown	Change Unknown	Start Unknown
Add To	Six children are playing tag in the yard. Three more children come to play. How many children are playing in the yard now? *Situation and Solution Equation*[1]*:* $6 + 3 = \square$	Six children are playing tag in the yard. Some more children come to play. Now there are 9 children in the yard. How many children came to play? *Situation Equation:* $6 + \square = 9$ *Solution Equation:* $9 - 6 = \square$	Some children are playing tag in the yard. Three more children come to play. Now there are 9 children in the yard. How many children were in the yard at first? *Situation Equation:* $\square + 3 = 9$ *Solution Equation:* $9 - 3 = \square$
Take From	Jake has 10 trading cards. He gives 3 to his brother. How many trading cards does he have left? *Situation and Solution Equation:* $10 - 3 = \square$	Jake has 10 trading cards. He gives some to his brother. Now Jake has 7 trading cards left. How many cards does he give to his brother? *Situation Equation:* $10 - \square = 7$ *Solution Equation:* $10 - 7 = \square$	Jake has some trading cards. He gives 3 to his brother. Now Jake has 7 trading cards left. How many cards does he start with? *Situation Equation:* $\square - 3 = 7$ *Solution Equation:* $7 + 3 = \square$

[1]A situation equation represents the structure (action) in the problem situation. A solution equation shows the operation used to find the answer.

Problem Types

Addition and Subtraction Problem Types (continued)

	Total Unknown	Addend Unknown	Other Addend Unknown
Put Together/ Take Apart	There are 9 red roses and 4 yellow roses in a vase. How many roses are in the vase? *Math Drawing*[2]: A math mountain with an empty box on top branching to 9 and 4. *Situation and Solution Equation:* $9 + 4 = \square$	Thirteen roses are in the vase. 9 are red and the rest are yellow. How many roses are yellow? *Math Drawing:* A math mountain with 13 on top branching to 9 and an empty box. *Situation Equation:* $13 = 9 + \square$ *Solution Equation:* $13 - 9 = \square$	Thirteen roses are in the vase. Some are red and 4 are yellow. How many are red? *Math Drawing:* A math mountain with 13 on top branching to an empty box and 4. *Situation Equation:* $13 = \square + 4$ *Solution Equation:* $13 - 4 = \square$

Both Addends Unknown is a productive extension of this basic situation, especially for small numbers less than or equal to 10. Such take apart situations can be used to show all the decompositions of a given number. The associated equations, which have the total on the left of the equal sign, help children understand that the = sign does not always mean makes or results in but always does mean is the same number as.

Both Addends Unknown

Ana has 13 roses. How many can she put in her red vase and how many in her blue vase?

Math Drawing:

A math mountain with 13 on top branching to two empty boxes.

Situation Equation:
$13 = \square + \square$

[2]These math drawings are called Math Mountains in Grades 1–3 and break-apart drawings in Grades 4 and 5.

Addition and Subtraction Problem Types (continued)

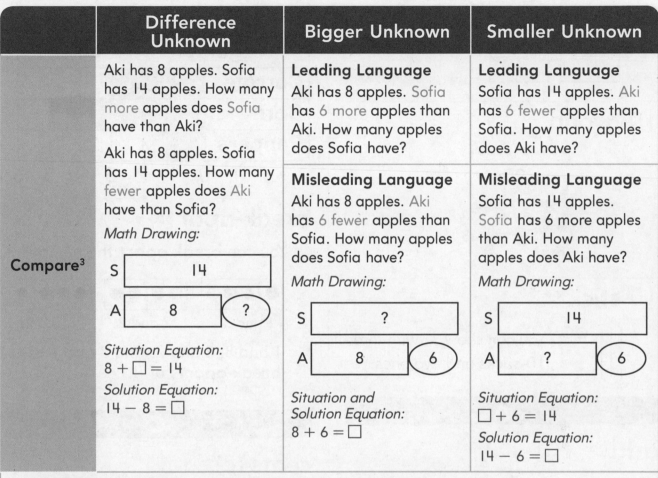

	Difference Unknown	Bigger Unknown	Smaller Unknown
Compare[3]	Aki has 8 apples. Sofia has 14 apples. How many more apples does Sofia have than Aki? Aki has 8 apples. Sofia has 14 apples. How many fewer apples does Aki have than Sofia? *Math Drawing:* S [14] A [8] (?) *Situation Equation:* $8 + \square = 14$ *Solution Equation:* $14 - 8 = \square$	**Leading Language** Aki has 8 apples. Sofia has 6 more apples than Aki. How many apples does Sofia have? **Misleading Language** Aki has 8 apples. Aki has 6 fewer apples than Sofia. How many apples does Sofia have? *Math Drawing:* S [?] A [8] (6) *Situation and Solution Equation:* $8 + 6 = \square$	**Leading Language** Sofia has 14 apples. Aki has 6 fewer apples than Sofia. How many apples does Aki have? **Misleading Language** Sofia has 14 apples. Sofia has 6 more apples than Aki. How many apples does Aki have? *Math Drawing:* S [14] A [?] (6) *Situation Equation:* $\square + 6 = 14$ *Solution Equation:* $14 - 6 = \square$

[3]A comparison sentence can always be said in two ways. One way uses *more*, and the other uses *fewer* or *less*. Misleading language suggests the wrong operation. For example, it says *Aki has 6 fewer apples than Sofia*, but you have to add 6 to Aki's 8 apples to get 14 apples.

5-group*

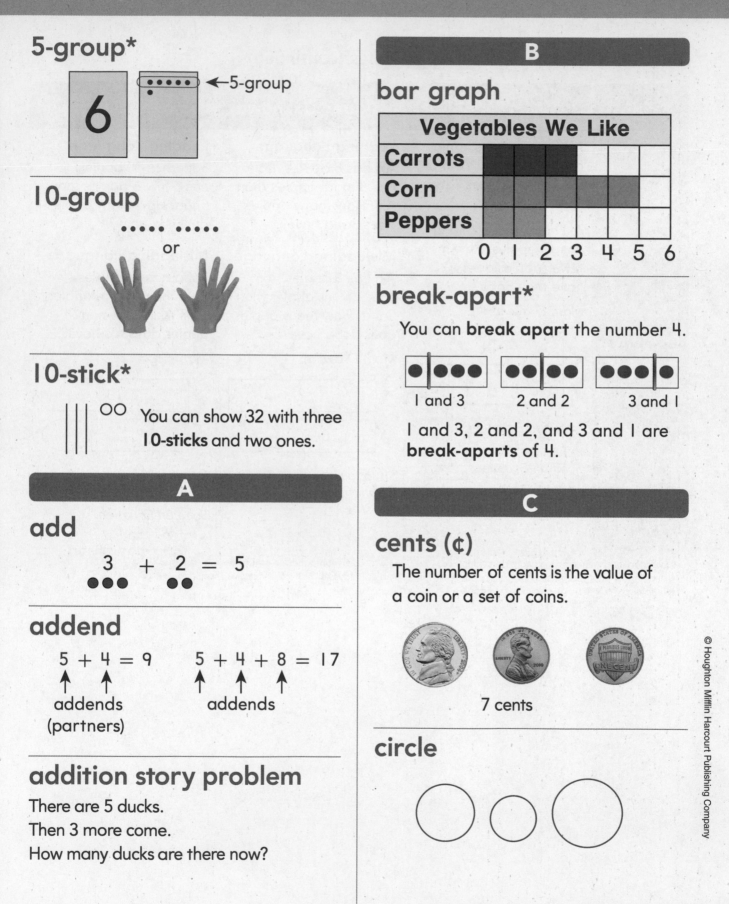

6 ←5-group

10-group

····· ·····

or

10-stick*

OO You can show 32 with three **10-sticks** and two ones.

add

3 + 2 = 5

addend

5 + 4 = 9   5 + 4 + 8 = 17

addends
(partners)   addends

addition story problem

There are 5 ducks.
Then 3 more come.
How many ducks are there now?

B

bar graph

Vegetables We Like

	0	1	2	3	4	5	6
Carrots							
Corn							
Peppers							

0 1 2 3 4 5 6

break-apart*

You can **break apart** the number 4.

1 and 3   2 and 2   3 and 1

1 and 3, 2 and 2, and 3 and 1 are **break-aparts** of 4.

C

cents (¢)

The number of cents is the value of a coin or a set of coins.

7 cents

circle

*A classroom research-based term developed for *Math Expressions*

circle drawing*

$$3 + 4$$
ooo | oooo

7

$$9 - 5$$
ooooo | oooo

4

clock

analog
clock

digital
clock

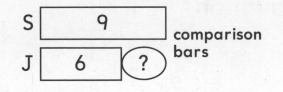
12:30

column

1	11	21	31	41	51	61	71	81	91
2	12	22	32	42	52	62	72	82	92
3	13	23	33	43	53	63	73	83	93
4	14	24	34	44	54	64	74	84	94
5	15	25	35	45	55	65	75	85	95
6	16	26	36	46	56	66	76	86	96
7	17	27	37	47	57	67	77	87	97
8	18	28	38	48	58	68	78	88	98
9	19	29	39	49	59	69	79	89	99
10	20	30	40	50	60	70	80	90	100

compare

You can **compare** numbers.

11 is less than 12.

$$11 < 12$$

12 is greater than 11.

$$12 > 11$$

You can **compare** objects by length.

The crayon is shorter than the pencil.
The pencil is longer than the crayon.

comparison bars*

Joe has 6 roses. Sasha has 9 roses.
How many more roses does Sasha have
than Joe?

S | 9
J | 6 | ?

comparison
bars

cone

---

*A classroom research-based term developed for *Math Expressions*

Glossary

corner

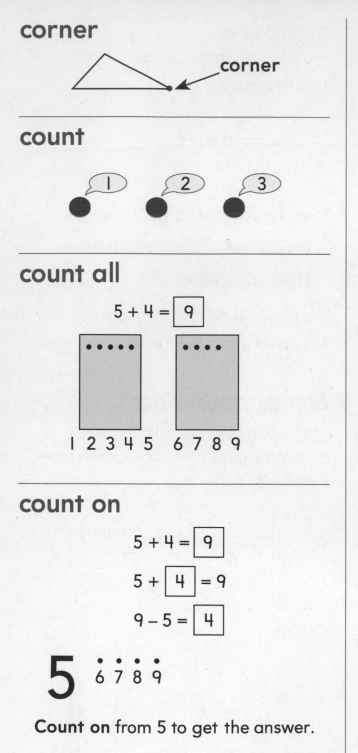

corner

count

count all

$$5 + 4 = \boxed{9}$$

1 2 3 4 5   6 7 8 9

count on

$$5 + 4 = \boxed{9}$$

$$5 + \boxed{4} = 9$$

$$9 - 5 = \boxed{4}$$

5 6 7 8 9

Count on from 5 to get the answer.

cube

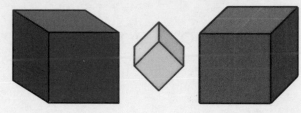

cylinder

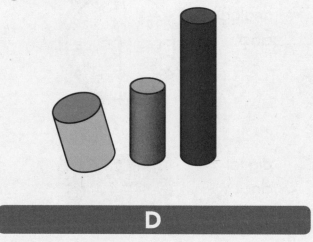

D

data

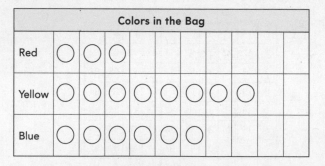

Colors in the Bag								
Red	○	○	○					
Yellow	○	○	○	○	○	○	○	○
Blue	○	○	○	○	○	○		

The **data** show how many of each color.

decade numbers

10, 20, 30, 40, 50, 60, 70, 80, 90

*A classroom research-based term developed for *Math Expressions*

difference

$$11 - 3 = 8$$

$$\begin{array}{r} 11 \\ -\ 3 \\ \hline 8 \end{array}$$

difference → 8

digit

15 is a 2-**digit** number.

The 1 in 15 means 1 ten.

The 5 in 15 means 5 ones.

dime

front   back

10 cents or 10¢

dot array

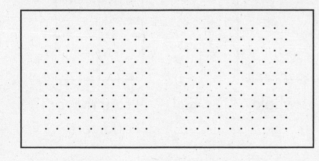

doubles

$$4 + 4 = 8$$

Both partners are the same.
They are doubles.

doubles minus 1

$7 + 7 = 14$, so

$7 + 6 = 13$, 1 less than 14.

doubles minus 2

$7 + 7 = 14$, so

$7 + 5 = 12$, 2 less than 14.

doubles plus 1

$6 + 6 = 12$, so

$6 + 7 = 13$, 1 more than 12.

doubles plus 2

$6 + 6 = 12$, so

$6 + 8 = 14$, 2 more than 12.

E

edge

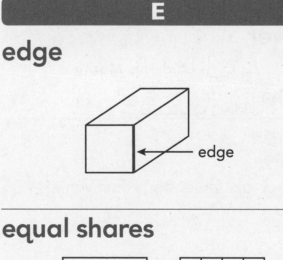

edge

equal shares

2 equal shares   4 equal shares

These show **equal shares.**

equal to (=)

$$4 + 4 = 8$$

4 plus 4 is **equal to** 8.

equation

$$4 + 3 = 7 \qquad 7 = 4 + 3$$

$$9 - 5 = 4 \qquad 4 = 9 - 5$$

F

face

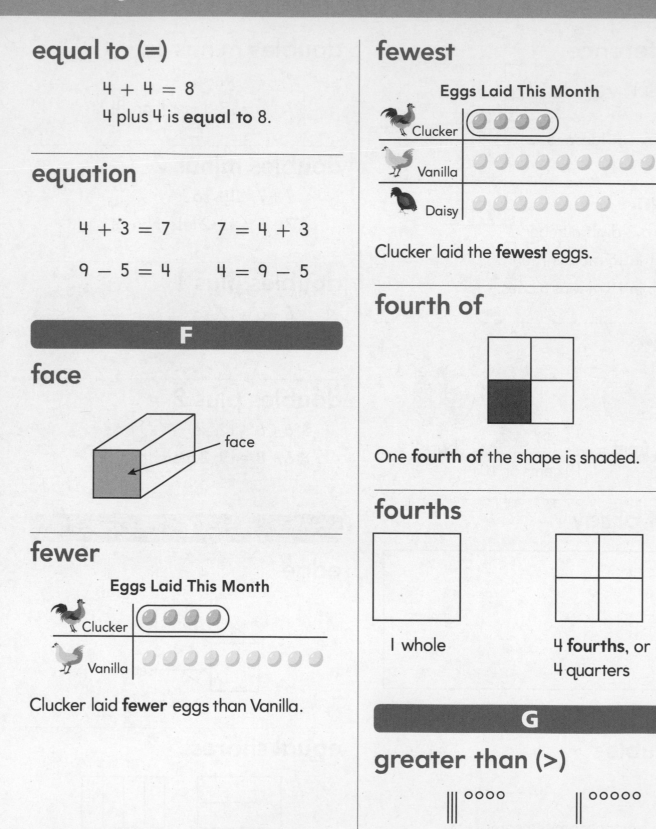

face

fewer

Eggs Laid This Month

| Clucker | 🥚🥚🥚🥚 |
| Vanilla | 🥚🥚🥚🥚🥚🥚🥚🥚 |

Clucker laid **fewer** eggs than Vanilla.

fewest

Eggs Laid This Month

Clucker	🥚🥚🥚🥚
Vanilla	🥚🥚🥚🥚🥚🥚🥚🥚
Daisy	🥚🥚🥚🥚🥚🥚

Clucker laid the **fewest** eggs.

fourth of

One **fourth of** the shape is shaded.

fourths

I whole

4 **fourths**, or
4 quarters

G

greater than (>)

|||°°°° ||°°°°°

34   >   25

34 is **greater than** 25.

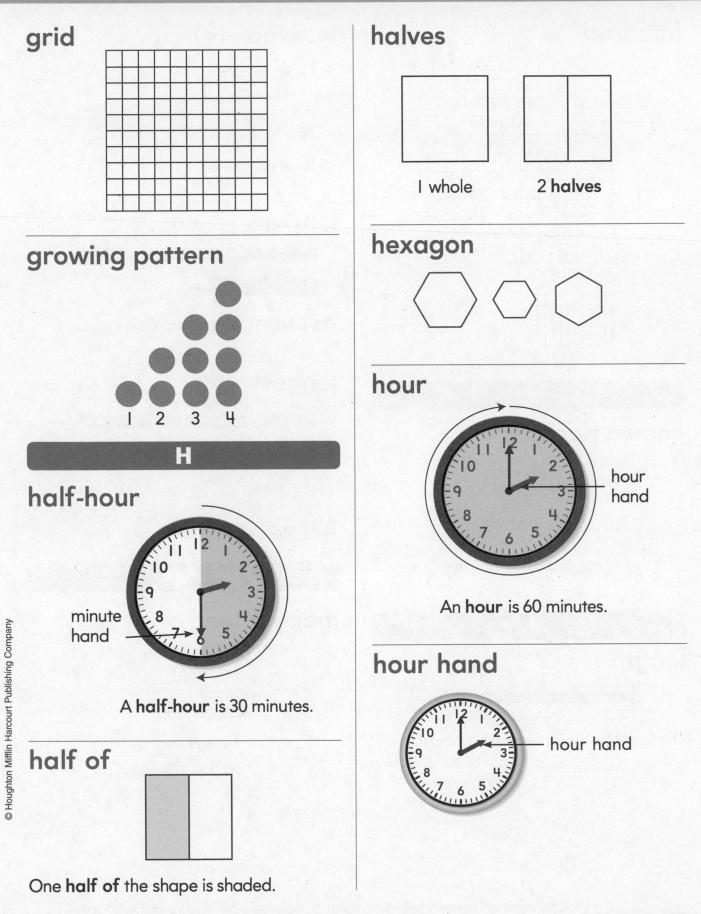

grid

growing pattern

1   2   3   4

H

half-hour

minute hand

A **half-hour** is 30 minutes.

half of

One **half of** the shape is shaded.

halves

1 whole   2 **halves**

hexagon

hour

hour hand

An **hour** is 60 minutes.

hour hand

hour hand

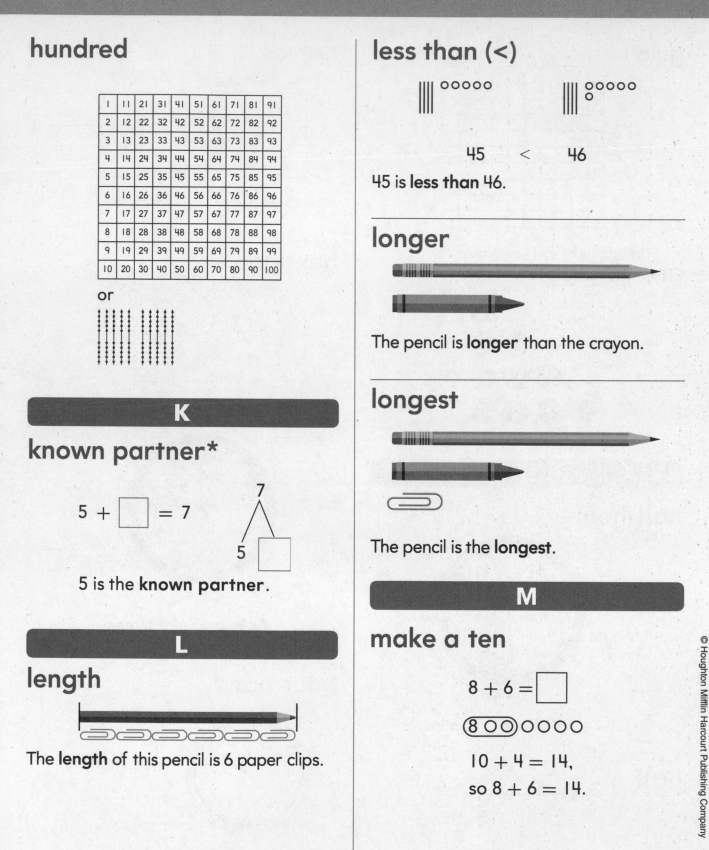

hundred

1	11	21	31	41	51	61	71	81	91
2	12	22	32	42	52	62	72	82	92
3	13	23	33	43	53	63	73	83	93
4	14	24	34	44	54	64	74	84	94
5	15	25	35	45	55	65	75	85	95
6	16	26	36	46	56	66	76	86	96
7	17	27	37	47	57	67	77	87	97
8	18	28	38	48	58	68	78	88	98
9	19	29	39	49	59	69	79	89	99
10	20	30	40	50	60	70	80	90	100

or

K

known partner*

$$5 + \boxed{} = 7$$

5 is the **known partner**.

L

length

The **length** of this pencil is 6 paper clips.

less than (<)

$$45 \quad < \quad 46$$

45 is **less than** 46.

longer

The pencil is **longer** than the crayon.

longest

The pencil is the **longest**.

M

make a ten

$$8 + 6 = \boxed{}$$

10 + 4 = 14,
so 8 + 6 = 14.

*A classroom research-based term developed for *Math Expressions*

Math Mountain*

$$8 \leftarrow \text{total}$$

$$\text{partner} \rightarrow 5 \quad 3 \leftarrow \text{partner}$$

measure

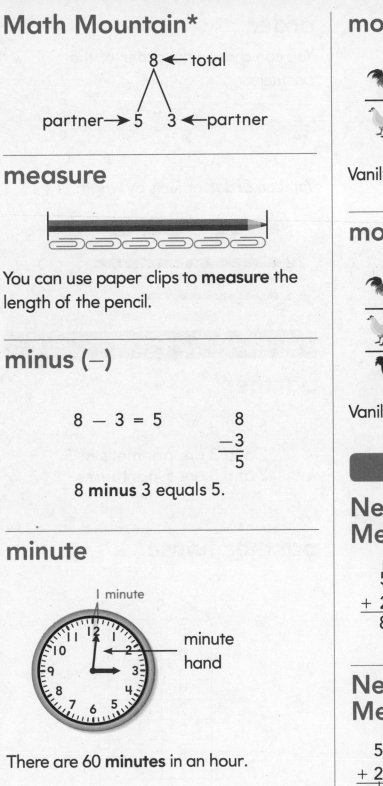

You can use paper clips to **measure** the length of the pencil.

minus (−)

$$8 - 3 = 5 \qquad \begin{array}{r} 8 \\ -3 \\ \hline 5 \end{array}$$

8 **minus** 3 equals 5.

minute

I minute

minute hand

There are 60 **minutes** in an hour.

more

Eggs Laid This Month

Clucker

Vanilla

Vanilla laid **more** eggs than Clucker.

most

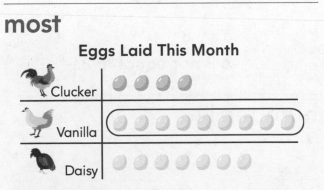

Eggs Laid This Month

Clucker

Vanilla

Daisy

Vanilla laid the **most** eggs.

N

New Group Above Method*

$$\begin{array}{r} {}^{1}56 \\ +28 \\ \hline 84 \end{array}$$

$6 + 8 = 14$
The 1 new ten in 14 goes up to the tens place.

New Group Below Method*

$$\begin{array}{r} 56 \\ +28 \\ \hline 84 \end{array}$$

$6 + 8 = 14$
The 1 new ten in 14 goes below in the tens place.

*A classroom research-based term developed for *Math Expressions*

nickel

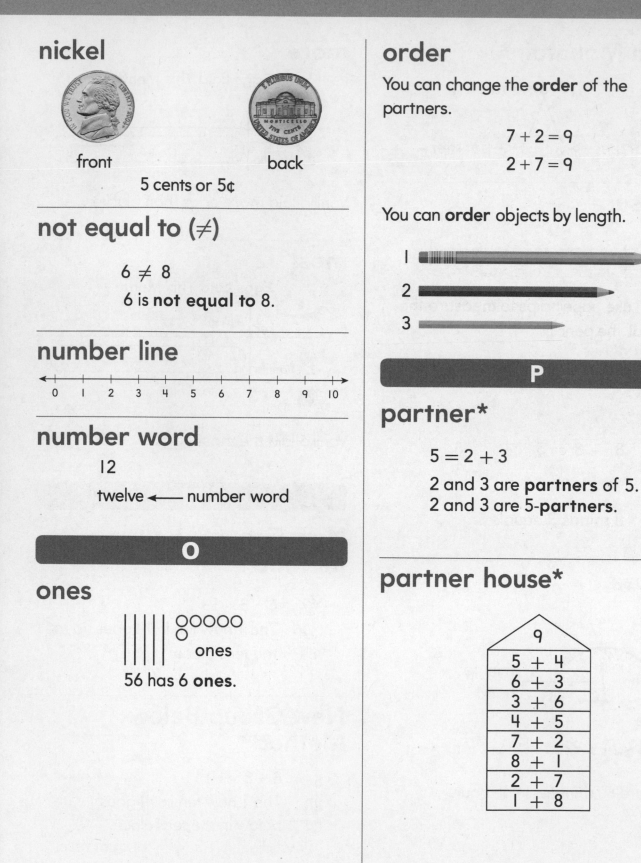

front   back

5 cents or 5¢

not equal to (≠)

$6 \neq 8$

6 is **not equal to** 8.

number line

0 1 2 3 4 5 6 7 8 9 10

number word

12

twelve ← number word

O

ones

| | | | | ○○○○○
○ ones

56 has 6 **ones**.

order

You can change the **order** of the partners.

$7 + 2 = 9$

$2 + 7 = 9$

You can **order** objects by length.

1

2

3

P

partner*

$5 = 2 + 3$

2 and 3 are **partners** of 5.
2 and 3 are 5-**partners**.

partner house*

9
5 + 4
6 + 3
3 + 6
4 + 5
7 + 2
8 + 1
2 + 7
1 + 8

*A classroom research-based term developed for *Math Expressions*

partner train*

4-train

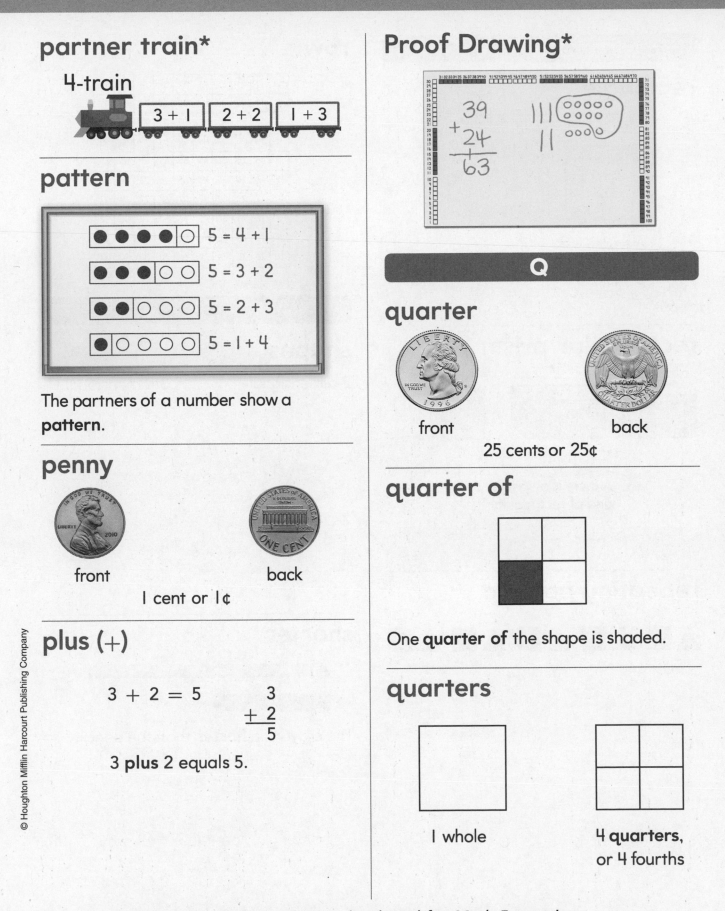

3 + 1   2 + 2   1 + 3

pattern

●●●● ○   5 = 4 + 1

●●● ○○   5 = 3 + 2

●● ○○○   5 = 2 + 3

● ○○○○   5 = 1 + 4

The partners of a number show a **pattern**.

penny

front   back

1 cent or 1¢

plus (+)

$$3 + 2 = 5 \qquad \begin{array}{r} 3 \\ + 2 \\ \hline 5 \end{array}$$

3 **plus** 2 equals 5.

Proof Drawing*

$$\begin{array}{r} 39 \\ + 24 \\ \hline 63 \end{array}$$

Q

quarter

front   back

25 cents or 25¢

quarter of

One **quarter of** the shape is shaded.

quarters

1 whole   4 **quarters**,
              or 4 fourths

*A classroom research-based term developed for *Math Expressions*

R

rectangle

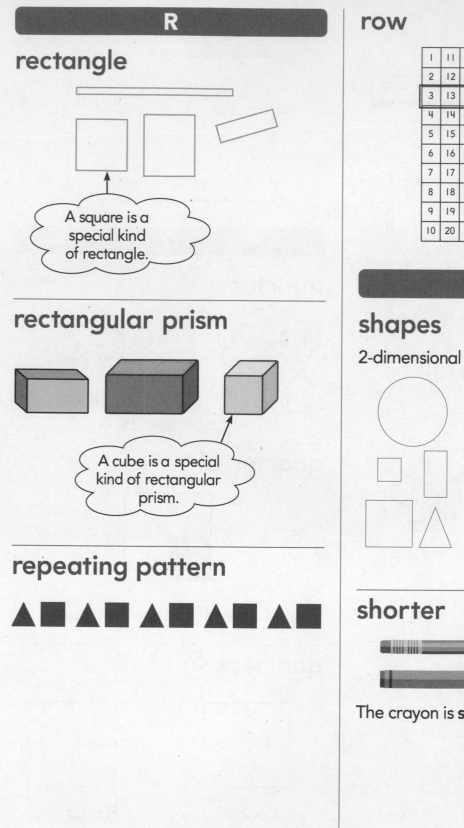

A square is a special kind of rectangle.

rectangular prism

A cube is a special kind of rectangular prism.

repeating pattern

row

1	11	21	31	41	51	61	71	81	91
2	12	22	32	42	52	62	72	82	92
3	13	23	33	43	53	63	73	83	93
4	14	24	34	44	54	64	74	84	94
5	15	25	35	45	55	65	75	85	95
6	16	26	36	46	56	66	76	86	96
7	17	27	37	47	57	67	77	87	97
8	18	28	38	48	58	68	78	88	98
9	19	29	39	49	59	69	79	89	99
10	20	30	40	50	60	70	80	90	100

S

shapes

2-dimensional

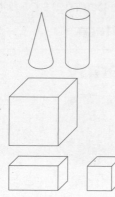

3-dimensional

shorter

The crayon is **shorter** than the pencil.

*A classroom research-based term developed for *Math Expressions*

shortest

The paper clip is the **shortest**.

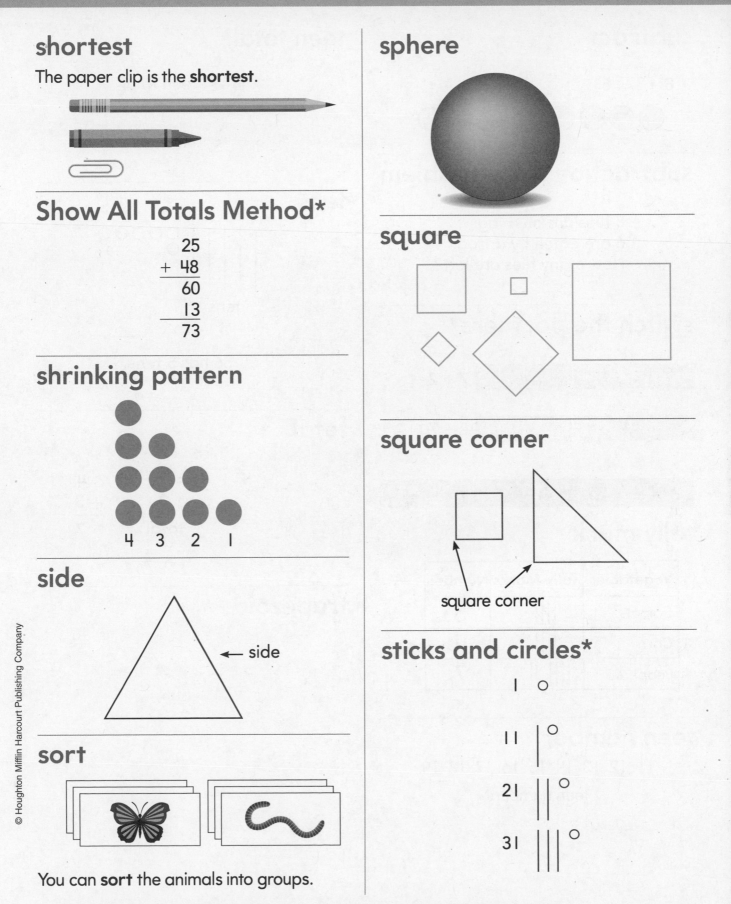

Show All Totals Method*

$$
\begin{array}{r}
25 \\
+\ 48 \\
\hline
60 \\
13 \\
\hline
73
\end{array}
$$

shrinking pattern

4   3   2   1

side

side

sort

You can **sort** the animals into groups.

sphere

square

square corner

square corner

sticks and circles*

1   ○

11 | ○

21 || ○

31 ||| ○

*A classroom research-based term developed for *Math Expressions*

subtract

$$8 - 3 = 5$$

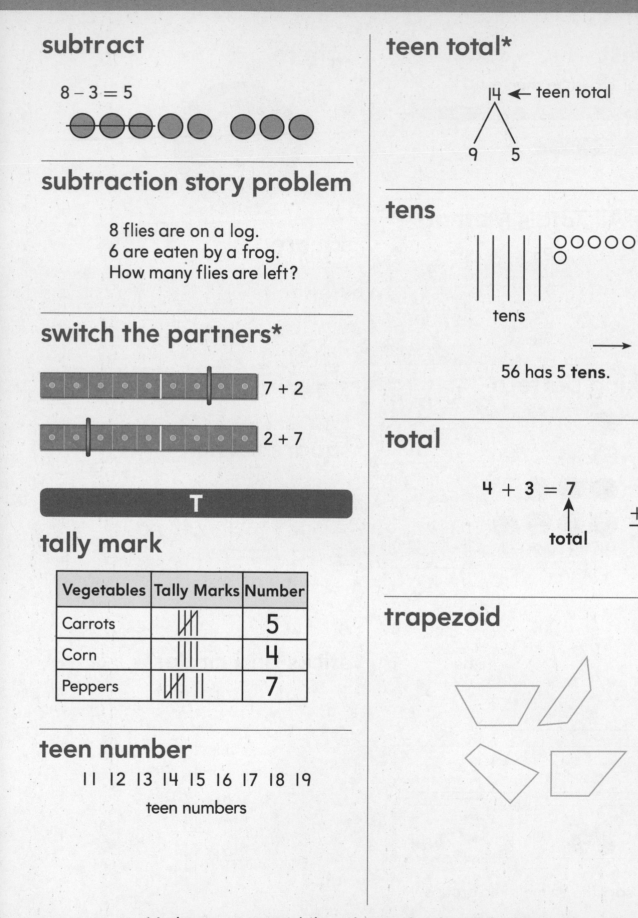

subtraction story problem

8 flies are on a log.
6 are eaten by a frog.
How many flies are left?

switch the partners*

7 + 2

2 + 7

T

tally mark

Vegetables	Tally Marks	Number
Carrots	⫴⃥	5
Corn	⫴⃒	4
Peppers	⫴⃥ ⎮⎮	7

teen number

11 12 13 14 15 16 17 18 19

teen numbers

teen total*

14 ← teen total

9   5

tens

tens

→

56 has 5 **tens**.

total

$$4 + 3 = 7$$

total

$$\begin{array}{r} 4 \\ +3 \\ \hline 7 \end{array}$$

trapezoid

*A classroom research-based term developed for *Math Expressions*

triangle

U

unknown partner*

7

4 ▢

4 + ▢ = 7

unknown total*

▢

5 3   5 + 3 = ▢

V

vertex

vertex

vertical form

$$\begin{array}{r} 6 \\ + 3 \\ \hline 9 \end{array} \qquad \begin{array}{r} 9 \\ - 3 \\ \hline 6 \end{array}$$

Z

zero

There are **zero** apples on the plate.

© Houghton Mifflin Harcourt Publishing Company

*A classroom research-based term developed for *Math Expressions*

1.ARO Algebraic Reasoning and Operations

1.ARO.1	Solve addition and subtraction word problems that involve adding to, putting together, taking from, taking apart, and comparing and have unknown quantities in all positions; represent problems using words, objects, drawings, length-based models (connecting cubes), numerals, number lines, as well as equations with a symbol for the unknown quantity.	Unit 1 Lessons 2, 3, 4, 5, 6, 7, 8; Unit 2 Lessons 1, 2, 3, 4, 6, 8, 10, 11, 12, 13, 14, 15, 16; Unit 3 Lessons 2, 3, 4, 5, 6, 7, 8, 9, 10, 11, 12; Unit 4 Lesson 5; Unit 5 Lessons 1, 2, 3, 4, 5, 11; Unit 6 Lessons 1, 2, 3, 4, 5, 6, 7, 8, 9
1.ARO.2	Solve addition word problems that involve three addends with a sum less than or equal to 20; represent a problem using objects or pictures or other methods, and equations that have a symbol for the unknown quantity.	Unit 5 Lessons 6, 11; Unit 6 Lessons 1, 4, 5, 9
1.ARO.3	Add and subtract applying the properties of operations.	Unit 1 Lessons 3, 4, 5, 6, 7, 8, 9; Unit 2 Lessons 7, 8, 9, 13; Unit 3 Lesson 5; Unit 4 Lessons 5, 10; Unit 5 Lessons 4, 6
1.ARO.4	Understand that a subtraction problem can be thought of as an unknown addend situation.	Unit 3 Lessons 6, 7, 8, 9, 10, 12; Unit 5 Lessons 2, 5, 10
1.ARO.5	Recognize the relationship between addition/subtraction and counting and understand that counting strategies can be used to add and subtract.	Unit 1 Lessons 1, 2, 3, 4, 9; Unit 2 Lessons 5, 6, 7, 8, 9; Unit 3 Lessons 1, 3, 4, 6, 7, 11; Unit 4 Lessons 1, 4, 5, 7, 15, 16, 17; Unit 5 Lessons 1, 2, 4

1.ARO.6	Fluently add and subtract through 10. Know how to add and subtract through 20 using strategies such as: for addition, *count on; make a ten* (example: $7 + 5 = 7 + 3 + 2$, so $7 + 3 + 2 = 10 + 2$, and $10 + 2 = 12$); *make an easier equal sum* (example: $9 + 6 = ?$, think $9 + 1 + 5 = 10 + 5$, so $10 + 5 = 15$; for subtraction, *decompose a number to get ten* (example: $17 - 8 = 17 - 7 - 1$, think $17 - 7 = 10$ and $10 - 1 = 9$); *use a related addition to subtract* (example: if you know $5 + 6 = 11$, then you can find $11 - 5 = 6$).	Unit 1 Lessons 3, 4, 5, 6, 7, 8, 9; Unit 2 Lessons 1, 2, 3, 5, 6, 7, 8, 9, 10, 11, 12, 13, 14, 15, 16; Unit 3 Lessons 1, 3, 4, 5, 6, 7, 10, 12; Unit 4 Lessons 4, 5, 6, 10, 15; Unit 5 Lessons 1, 2, 3, 4, 5, 10, 11; Unit 6 Lessons 3, 8; Unit 7 Lessons 5, 8, 13; Unit 8 Lesson 5
1.ARO.7	Know the meaning of the equal sign; decide whether or not an equation that involves addition or subtraction is true or false.	Unit 2 Lessons 3, 4, 11, 12, 13, 16; Unit 3 Lesson 12; Unit 5 Lesson 11
1.ARO.8	Find the unknown number in an addition or subtraction equation (examples: $9 + ? = 12$; $8 = ? - 5$; $7 + 2 = ?$).	Unit 1 Lessons 3, 4, 5, 6, 7, 8; Unit 2 Lessons 5, 6, 7, 8, 9, 10, 12, 13, 14, 16; Unit 3 Lessons 3, 4, 5, 6, 7, 8, 9, 11, 12; Unit 4 Lessons 4, 5, 6, 10, 13, 14, 15, 16; Unit 5 Lessons 1, 2, 3, 4, 5, 10; Unit 6 Lessons 6, 7
1.ARO.9	Create simple patterns using objects, pictures, numbers and rules. Identify possible rules to complete or extend patterns. Patterns may be repeating, growing or shrinking. Calculators can be used to create and explore patterns.	Unit 1 Lessons 10, 11; Unit 5 Lesson 9

1.PVO Place Value and Operations

1.PVO.1	Count, with or without objects, forward and backward to 120, starting at any number less than 120. For the number sequence to 120, read and write the corresponding numerals; represent a group of objects with a written numeral, addition and subtraction, pictures, tally marks, number lines and manipulatives, such as bundles of sticks and base 10 blocks. Skip count by 2s, 5s, and 10s.	Unit 4 Lessons 1, 2, 7, 8, 9, 10, 11, 15, 16, 18; Unit 5 Lessons 7, 8, 9; Unit 6 Lessons 4, 5

Mathematical Standards

1.PVO.2	For a two-digit number, understand that the digit to the right represents ones and the digit to the left represents tens.	Unit 4 Lessons 1, 2, 3, 4, 7, 8, 9, 10, 11, 12, 13, 14, 16, 17, 18; Unit 5 Lessons 7, 8, 9; Unit 8 Lesson 1
1.PVO.2.a	Understand that 10 can be thought of as a group of ten ones named *ten*.	Unit 4 Lessons 1, 2, 3, 4, 9, 10, 16, 18; Unit 5 Lessons 8, 10; Unit 8 Lesson 1
1.PVO.2.b	Understand that the numbers 11 through 19 are made up of one ten and one through nine ones.	Unit 4 Lessons 2, 3, 4, 5, 8, 10; Unit 5 Lesson 8
1.PVO.2.c	Know that the decade numbers 10 through 90 represent one through nine tens and zero ones.	Unit 4 Lessons 1, 7, 8, 9, 13, 14, 18; Unit 5 Lesson 10; Unit 8 Lesson 1
1.PVO.3	Apply place value concepts to compare two 2-digit numbers using the symbols >, <, and =.	Unit 4 Lessons 3, 12, 16, 18; Unit 8 Lesson 6
1.PVO.4	Add numbers through 100, such as a two-digit number and a one-digit number or a two-digit number and a multiple of ten. Understand that groups of objects or drawings and strategies can be used to find sums (examples of strategies: *relationship between addition and subtraction, place value, properties of operations*) and explain how the strategy and recorded result are related. Know that to add two-digit numbers, ones are added to ones and tens are added to tens and in some instances, ten ones will result in making one ten.	Unit 4 Lessons 9, 10, 11, 13, 14, 15, 16, 17, 18; Unit 5 Lessons 9, 10, 11; Unit 8 Lessons 1, 2, 3, 4, 5, 6
1.PVO.5	Use mental math to find a number that is 10 more or 10 less than any given two-digit number (without using counting) and explain the reasoning used to find the result.	Unit 5 Lessons 8, 9
1.PVO.6	For numbers 10 through 90, subtract multiples of 10 resulting in differences of 0 through 80. Use groups of objects or pictures and strategies to subtract. Strategies can include place value concepts, the relationship between addition and subtraction, and properties of operations. Explain how the strategy and recorded result are related.	Unit 5 Lessons 9, 10, 11; Unit 8 Lesson 6

1.MDA Measurement and Data Analysis

1.MDA.1	Compare to order three items by length. Compare the lengths of two items using a third item (indirect comparison).	Unit 7 Lessons 12, 14
1.MDA.2	Determine the length of an object by placing as many same-size smaller units end-to-end as needed along the span of the object ensuring no gaps or overlaps. Understand that length of the object is the number of same-size units that were used. (Note: The number of "length-units" should not extend beyond the end of the object being measured.)	Unit 7 Lessons 13, 14
1.MDA.3	Use analog and digital clocks to express time orally and in written form in hours and half-hours.	Unit 7 Lessons 1, 2, 3, 4, 5, 14
1.MDA.4	Organize, represent, and interpret data with up to three categories using picture graphs, bar graphs, and tally charts. Ask questions and provide answers about how many in all comprise the data and how many are in each category. Compare the number in one category to that in another category.	Unit 6 Lessons 1, 2, 3, 4, 5, 9
1.MDA.5	Recognize and identify coins (penny, nickel, dime, and quarter) and their value and use the ¢ (cent) symbol appropriately.	Unit 2 Lesson 7; Unit 4, Lessons 8, 19, 20
1.MDA.6	Know the comparative values of all U.S. coins (e.g. a dime is of greater value than a nickel). Find equivalent values (e.g., a nickel is equivalent to 5 pennies.) Solve problems and use the values of the coins in the solutions of the problems.	Unit 2 Lesson 7; Unit 4 Lessons 8, 19, 20
1.MDA.7	Explore dimes and pennies as they relate to place value concepts.	Unit 4 Lessons 8, 19, 20

1.GSR Geometry and Spatial Reasoning

1.GSR.1	Understand the difference between defining attributes of a figure (examples: a square has 4 sides of equal length and 4 vertices) and non-defining attributes (examples: size, color, position). Using concrete materials and paper and pencil, build and draw geometric figures according to their defining attributes.	Unit 7 Lessons 6, 7, 8, 9, 10
1.GSR.2	Create composite geometric figures by putting together two-dimensional figures (triangles, squares, rectangles, trapezoids, half-circles, and quarter-circles) or three-dimensional figures (cubes, rectangular prisms, cylinders, and cones), then form a new figure from the composite figure.	Unit 7 Lessons 9, 10, 11
1.GSR.3	Separate rectangles and circles into two or four equal shares, and use the words *halves, fourths,* and *quarters,* and the phrases *half of, fourth of,* and *quarter of* to identify the equal-size shares. Use the terms "two of" or " four of" to describe the number of equal shares in the whole. Understand that when a figure is separated into more equal shares, the size of the shares is smaller.	Unit 7 Lessons 8, 9, 14

Mathematical Processes and Practices

MPP1	
Problem Solving	Unit 1 Lessons 2, 3, 4, 6, 8, 9, 10, 11 Unit 2 Lessons 1, 2, 3, 4, 6, 7, 8, 9, 10, 13, 14, 16 Unit 3 Lessons 1, 2, 3, 4, 6, 7, 8, 9, 10, 11, 12 Unit 4 Lessons 2, 3, 5, 10, 18, 19, 20 Unit 5 Lessons 1, 2, 3, 4, 5, 6, 9, 11 Unit 6 Lessons 1, 2, 4, 5, 6, 7, 8, 9 Unit 7 Lessons 8, 12, 14 Unit 8 Lessons 1, 3, 4, 6
MPP2	
Abstract and Quantitative Reasoning	Unit 1 Lessons 3, 4, 5, 6, 7, 8, 9 Unit 2 Lessons 1, 2, 3, 4, 6, 10, 11, 12, 13, 15, 16 Unit 3 Lessons 3, 5, 6, 12 Unit 4 Lessons 1, 3, 4, 6, 7, 8, 9, 10, 11, 12, 14, 15, 16, 17, 18, 19 Unit 5 Lessons 1, 2, 3, 4, 5, 9, 10, 11 Unit 6 Lessons 1, 2, 3, 5, 6, 8, 9 Unit 7 Lessons 8, 9, 14 Unit 8 Lessons 1, 2, 3, 4, 5, 6
MPP3	
Use and Evaluate Logical Reasoning	Unit 1 Lessons 1, 2, 3, 4, 5, 6, 7, 8, 9, 10 Unit 2 Lessons 1, 2, 3, 4, 6, 7, 8, 9, 10, 11, 12, 13, 14, 16 Unit 3 Lessons 2, 3, 4, 6, 7, 8, 9, 10, 11, 12 Unit 4 Lessons 1, 2, 3, 4, 5, 6, 7, 8, 9, 10, 11, 12, 13, 14, 15, 16, 17, 18, 19, 20 Unit 5 Lessons 1, 2, 3, 4, 5, 6, 7, 8, 9, 10, 11 Unit 6 Lessons 1, 2, 3, 4, 5, 6, 7, 8, 9 Unit 7 Lessons 1, 2, 3, 4, 5, 6, 7, 8, 9, 10, 11, 12, 13, 14 Unit 8 Lessons 1, 2, 3, 4, 5, 6
MPP4	
Mathematical Modeling	Unit 1 Lessons 2, 3, 9 Unit 2 Lessons 1, 2, 6, 10, 13, 16 Unit 3 Lessons 1, 2, 5, 6, 7, 8, 9, 10, 11, 12 Unit 4 Lessons 2, 3, 4, 5, 10, 18, 19, 20 Unit 5 Lessons 1, 2, 3, 4, 6, 8, 9, 11 Unit 6 Lessons 2, 3, 4, 5, 6, 7, 8, 9 Unit 7 Lessons 3, 8, 12, 14 Unit 8 Lessons 1, 2, 3, 6

MPP5

Use Mathematical Tools

Unit 1 Lessons 1, 2, 3, 4, 5, 6, 7, 8, 9
Unit 2 Lessons 5, 6, 7, 8, 16
Unit 3 Lessons 1, 2, 3, 4, 7, 11
Unit 4 Lessons 1, 2, 3, 4, 5, 6, 7, 8, 9, 10, 11, 12, 13, 14, 16, 17, 18, 19
Unit 5 Lessons 1, 2, 6, 7, 8, 9, 10, 11
Unit 6 Lessons 3, 4, 5, 8, 9
Unit 7 Lessons 1, 2, 5, 6, 7, 8, 9, 10, 11, 12, 13, 14
Unit 8 Lessons 2, 3, 6

MPP6

Use Precise Mathematical Language

Unit 1 Lessons 1, 2, 3, 4, 5, 6, 7, 8, 9, 10
Unit 2 Lessons 1, 3, 4, 5, 6, 7, 8, 9, 10, 11, 12, 13, 14, 16
Unit 3 Lessons 1, 2, 3, 4, 5, 6, 7, 8, 9, 10, 11, 12
Unit 4 Lessons 1, 2, 3, 4, 5, 6, 7, 8, 9, 10, 11, 12, 13, 14, 15, 16, 17, 18, 19, 20
Unit 5 Lessons 1, 2, 3, 4, 5, 6, 7, 8, 9, 10, 11
Unit 6 Lessons 1, 2, 3, 4, 5, 6, 7, 8, 9
Unit 7 Lessons 1, 2, 3, 4, 5, 6, 7, 8, 9, 10, 11, 12, 13, 14
Unit 8 Lessons 1, 2, 3, 4, 5, 6

MPP7

See Structure

Unit 1 Lessons 1, 2, 3, 4, 5, 6, 7, 8, 9, 10, 11
Unit 2 Lessons 13, 14, 16
Unit 3 Lessons 1, 3, 9, 12
Unit 4 Lessons 1, 2, 3, 5, 6, 7, 8, 9, 10,13, 17, 18, 19
Unit 5 Lessons 1, 2, 3, 5, 6, 7, 8, 9, 10, 11
Unit 6 Lessons 6, 8, 9
Unit 7 Lessons 1, 2, 3, 4, 5, 6, 7, 9, 10, 11, 14
Unit 8 Lessons 2, 6

MPP8

Generalize

Unit 1 Lessons 1, 2, 3, 4, 5, 6, 7, 8, 9
Unit 2 Lessons 6, 7, 8, 11, 14, 16
Unit 3 Lessons 8, 9, 12
Unit 4 Lessons 1, 2, 5, 6, 7, 9, 10, 12, 13, 14, 15, 17, 18
Unit 5 Lessons 1, 2, 4, 5, 6, 7, 8, 9, 10, 11
Unit 6 Lessons 1, 6, 7, 9
Unit 7 Lessons 3, 6, 7, 8, 9, 10, 12, 14
Unit 8 Lessons 1, 2, 4, 6

Index

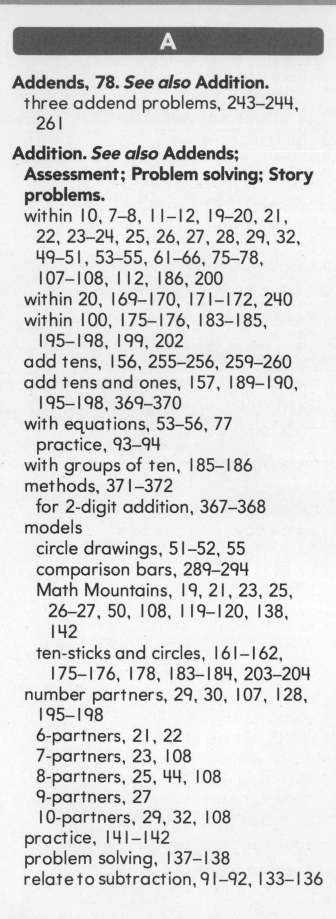

© Houghton Mifflin Harcourt Publishing Company

B

C

D

© Houghton Mifflin Harcourt Publishing Company

Index

Index

Index

Illustrator: Josh Brill

Did you ever try to use shapes to draw animals like the frog on the cover?

Over the last 10 years Josh has been using geometric shapes to design his animals. His aim is to keep the animal drawings simple and use color to make them appealing.

Add some color to the frog Josh drew. Then try drawing a cat or dog or some other animal using the shapes below.

Shape Toolbox